P9-CSU-900

Life Coach

22 Expert Coaches Help You Navigate
Life Challenges To Achieve Your Goals

Compiled by Kyra Schaefer

Life Coach: 22 Expert Coaches Help You Navigate Life Challenges To Achieve Your Goals

Copyright © 2019. All rights reserved. Each author in this book retains the copyright to their individual section. Their submissions are printed herein with their permission. Each author is responsible for their individual opinions expressed through their words. No part of this publication may be reproduced, distributed, or transmitted to any form or by any means, including photocopying, recording, or other electronic mechanical methods, without the prior written permission of the publisher.

As You Wish Publishing, LLC Kyra@asyouwishpublishing.com
602-592-1141

ISBN-13: 978-1-7324982-4-2

ISBN-10: 1-7324982-4-5

Library of Congress Control Number: 2019902530

Compiled by Kyra Schaefer

Edited by Todd Schaefer

Printed in the United States of America.

Nothing in this book or any affiliations with this book is a substitute for medical or psychological help. If you are needing help please seek it.

Michelle,
you are such a beautiful bright light.

Dedication

To all those who seek to make life better.

w/ love

Table of Contents

Foreword by Kyra Schaefer

How do you know you need a life coach?

You have been trying to get things done but are feeling defeated in your efforts. You can't seem to get motivated even though you know once you take some steps you will be happier. You have wanted to feel better, healthier and stronger but don't know how to get started.

"Life Coach" is designed with you in mind. The intention is to give you a life coach in your pocket to carry around with you. You will experience exercises to help you get unstuck in multiple areas. Everyone has gifts to share, and when you are bogged down by life challenges, it becomes challenging to realize your full potential. As you read the following pages, you have an opportunity to partner with the writers of this book in a way that helps you get past limitations and step more clearly into your desired future.

Several of the coaches in this book have helped me on my journey personally, and I can genuinely say they are the most compassionate, kind-hearted individuals you are likely ever to meet. That isn't to say they haven't asked me to get outside of my comfort zone or intently stood beside me encouraging my next leaps. We all need a champion for our highest good, even when we aren't sure what that looks like. Having a team of people to guide and support you is imperative as you go after your dreams.

Sometimes, we are uncertain of our dreams, our purpose or what will help us feel fulfilled. The authors address the issue of discovering your fulfillment and give you tools to consider using as you follow the next best step before you.

It also doesn't have to be difficult. Often, we look at self-reflection as a negative, believing if we look at the things holding us back, we will somehow feel overwhelmed and defeated. The truth is that once we look at ourselves in this way with a loving friend and coach, we can begin to transform that old limiting belief system and step into our truth.

A life coach doesn't fix you, and you aren't broken. You already have the power within you to create positive change. Your coach only reminds you of that fact. As you look at the issue you face with someone who is a helpmate, big miracles begin to happen. The things that held you back in the past will no longer affect your daily reality, and you will move more readily into the life you have been imagining. As a coach partners with you on your journey of self-knowing, your ego (that part of you that speaks negatively to you, aids in self-blame and discourages success) can no longer keep up the game that makes you feel less than others. The lies you have been telling yourself for years will begin to fade away.

When we begin to dismantle the belief systems that have been keeping us stuck, it can feel disorienting, and having a partner to guide us through this difficult time is essential to our success. Life coaches remind us of who we are and what is possible. The coaches in this book do so through each chapter as they guide you with personal stories, tools, and exercises to help you. The journey doesn't end at this book. This book may only be the beginning.

When you are ready, you may want to follow up with the authors in this book. Find the life coach you resonate with and reach out to them. Let them know you are ready to step up and take control of your life in a new way. If you already work with a coach, I have found it's helpful to learn from multiple sources. In this book, you are given variety and can connect with various people from different backgrounds to aid you in your success on this adventurous life.

How to use this book:

Trust your instincts and know you are on the right path. By simply picking up this book, you know there is some area that needs improvement in your life. You may flip to any page or chapter randomly, and the insight will flow to your current question. You may also go to any section and do its exercises. You will get to know the authors as they express their journey and how they came to this place in their lives that has caused them to take a leap of faith and offer encouragement to others.

However you choose to use this book, please know you are never alone in your endeavors. We have all been through something in our lives that has caused us to question or doubt ourselves, and now we have a resource we can turn to and create more possibility, more positivity and more integrity.

Thank you for taking the time to absorb the vast years of combined knowledge in this book. I can't begin to tell you how honored I am to be in the presence of such amazing people. They have made a difference in my life, and I hope that you gain new awareness in yours as well.

Kyra Schaefer is a bestselling author and publisher who has worked in the non-traditional healing field for 15 years. She has helped thousands of people on their self-discovery journeys through Clinical Hypnotherapy. Currently, Kyra owns As You

Wish Publishing and makes book publishing accessible for aspiring authors who want to write books that help. If you would like to be an author in her upcoming books or write a solo book of your own please visit her at www.asyouwishpublishing.com

CHAPTER

Embrace The Muck And Get Unstuck
By Ali Dombek Handel

ALI HANDEL

Ali Dombek Handel is a holistic life coach from Denver, Colorado. Ali has over 25 years of experience in the art forms of coaching, communications, relationships, business, and strategy. Ali works with clients who want to transition a life of chaos into one of peace, freedom, and bliss. Ali offers transformational life coaching programs intended to shift you radically out of your current state into a life aligned with your true essence. Ali teaches you life-changing skills that have far-reaching benefits. Ali meets you where you're at and inspires you to thrive no matter what your situation. Ali's multi-faceted experience, skills, and talents are what make her an exceptional coach.

Contact Ali today for a free coaching consultation:

303-817-3027

Visit: www.blissfulsol.com/ Email: blissfulsol@comcast.net

Acknowledgments

I would like to thank my kind and compassionate husband, Jason. His loving strength, while I was stuck in the muck, was integral to my healing journey. He believed in me when I didn't believe in myself. I would also like to thank my Martha Beck coaching tribe who continue to be a source of inspiration and growth. I am grateful to my clients who open their hearts to me, and through sharing their deep vulnerabilities are able to create a new way of being. Witnessing your transformation is why I do what I do and fills me with an incredible sense of reward. Finally, thank you to my dear friend and soul sister, Sarah Beth Brown who reviewed my article with a kind and honest perspective. Thank you all, from the bottom of my heart.

Embrace The Muck And Get Unstuck
By Ali Dombek Handel

Your life is made up of tiny deaths and rebirths. Consider the vast changes that happen between birth, adolescence, adulthood, and senior years. Remember that there are infinite stepping stones between those phases. All of this follows a transformative process. Bestselling author and life coach Martha Beck speaks about this process as being similar to the metamorphosis of a caterpillar into a butterfly: the death of the old cells through the meltdown and shedding of skin, the curing of the cellular goo inside the silky cocoon, and finally, the rebirthing of the chrysalis into the butterfly. As a human, you're melting down your old way of being so that you can make room for newness. This is a metaphorical death of your old limiting thoughts and perspectives. It can be frightening. That's why most people skip over the muck, numb the pain, and go on with their lives. But, why do you keep repeating the same patterns? Why are you still suffering? Consider that, in every moment, in all aspects of life, you're experiencing a metaphorical death and rebirth. Everything is in constant flux, and so are you.

The key to getting unstuck is to embrace where you are. It is in this mucky place where you will find the solution to your problems, the root cause of your suffering. As dark and scary as it may be, this is where you find your answers.

Trust me, I've been stuck. After spending nearly 23 years in the healthcare IT industry, and managing people for the last half, I had a *big* meltdown. In 2016, my normal happy-go-lucky and optimistic attitude began to diminish. I would walk home from work nearly every day in a puddle of tears. I didn't realize that I was disengaging from my teams. I didn't realize that I had shut my office door and made myself hidden. But, my teams did notice, and they shared this on my performance review. Receiving that blatant feedback was painful. Even my manager wondered what had happened since she agreed that it wasn't my normal way of being. I went from rock star to rock bottom in a matter of months. It was terrifying feeling stuck like this. Even more terrifying was not knowing why I sunk so low into the muck.

I resigned from my job in August of 2016 to focus on my health. My journey was one of healing and self-care. I toyed with following my dream of becoming a life coach and immersing in my life-long passion for leading transformational work. But, even with my desire being high, my motivation was missing. I was depressed, filled with unrelenting anxiety, and didn't know why. I've always been health-conscious, active, analytical, and engaged. However, throughout my life, I also suffered from a myriad of unexplained health issues like migraines, major hormone disruption, low immunity, food intolerances, and digestive issues. My co-workers referred to me as the sickest healthy person they knew. After I resigned, I made it my number one goal to heal from the inside out. I modified my diet as a first step, and that's when I started to experience a significant improvement. It was one piece to the larger puzzle of my emotional healing journey.

Later that year, while engaged in a life coaching session with a friend, I was able to identify one of the root causes of my emotional suffering. I subconsciously held a belief that "I'm not good enough." It seemed that no matter what I did growing up, I never did it well enough, and therefore, I couldn't be good enough. That's the story I told myself. That's the story I believed. That's also the story that led to a lack of confidence and more illness.

This belief was deeply woven into my being. By dissolving that limiting belief in that single coaching session, I felt a newfound spark of freedom and inner peace that I had never experienced; it was profound. That's when *everything* changed.

I enrolled in the Martha Beck Life Coaching Institute that next week. Throughout the nine-month intensive program, I discovered a number of additional core limiting beliefs and dissolved them too. I felt lighter than I had in my life. I started my coaching business and helped my clients move through their muck and past some serious blocks. I was simultaneously freeing myself and others of a limited mindset. I felt like a dragon slayer!

One of the unexpected benefits I experienced was a vast improvement to my overall health. This was tied to another limiting belief that "I should feel well." This seemed strange at first. Shouldn't everyone feel well? As a general sentiment, yes. But, in my reality, no; I hadn't felt well most of my life. Remember, my coworkers referred to me as the sickest healthy person they knew. By identifying this belief, I was finally able to accept the reality that it's okay not to feel well. What followed was extraordinary. I was finally able to relax and care for myself without guilt when I didn't feel well. Soon afterward, my migraines ceased, and so did my anxiety and depression.

Never in my wildest dreams did I think this could happen. I *healed myself.* Releasing my limited mindset and embracing my reality was the missing piece to the puzzle. It's amazing how believing a limited and false reality affected every aspect of my life.

This is a true story. This is my story. And, I hope it inspires you. So, how do you get unstuck?

Embrace the muck.

You must embrace the muck and get cozy in your cocoon. It's within the muck that you identify the root cause of your suffering, shed your skin, and birth new wings to fly with freedom.

Zen Buddhist and teacher Thich Nhat Hanh sums up this concept well in his metaphorical quote, "No mud, no lotus." He inspires us to embrace our suffering and transform it. In other words, it is only by remaining in the muck that the lotus can bloom.

Allow yourself to stay in the muck, and you too will find the answers to your problems. Be there even when you're frightened. Be there with intention. Be there as long as you need. And, trust that you will know when you're ready to emerge.

Get quiet and feel everything.

Getting quiet means spending some time free of your racing thoughts and worry about what might happen, and what once was. Yep, yogis, spiritual leaders, and inspirers have been on to something; they've mastered the art of getting quiet. The intent is to create a gap between the past and future and be in the *now*.

What to do: connect your mind and body.

Most of us have been so distracted by the chaos of life that we've become disconnected from our bodies. We're living in our heads and have forgotten about our physical bodies altogether. Can you relate?

Your physical body holds invaluable wisdom that acts as an alert system when something isn't aligned with your true essence. This can come in the form of physical pain, tension, and tightness, and can often manifest as widespread health issues. Connecting your mind and your physical body helps you to unlock the wisdom from your essential self. This requires you to get quiet so that you can *listen to* and *hear* these messages. When you get quiet, don't think of this as checking out, but rather checking into the deep and sacred wisdom that's there for you at any moment.

Take 5-10 minutes out of your day and practice this simple mind/body meditation. In this exercise, you will learn to scan your body for messages by focusing first on the physical sensations such as temperature, tingling, pulsing, numbness, pain, or fatigue, and then on any subconscious messages that may be revealed to you during the process. During the exercise, you will become an observer of your body and thoughts. With any meditation, you may become distracted. If this happens, bring your awareness back to your breath and then continue with the scan.

How to do it:

1. Lie down in a comfortable position.
2. Take a few long deep breaths allowing your breath to melt away any tension.
3. Focus on the air going into and out of your physical body parts with love and appreciation.
4. Scan each part of your body and notice whatever physical sensations you experience from your toes, calves, legs, spine, head, and then all the way out through your shoulders, arms, and fingertips.
5. Once you complete the scan, bring your awareness to the area of your body that needs your immediate attention (your mind will guide you there).
6. Describe that part of your body with three adjectives.
7. Ask that part what it needs from you.
8. Ask that part what it would like you to know.
9. Allow yourself to receive this wisdom.

You can do this scan any time or place throughout your day. A good time to do this is just before bed as it helps you to remember to do it (think of it as a bedtime prayer). It also supports a routine that enables relaxation that can prepare you for a restful sleep.

Question everything and identify the problem.

You may not know why your life seems to be stuck, so how could you possibly know how to move forward? You can say all the positive affirmations you like, set lofty goals, and make all the plans, but if you don't know the true reason your life is a mess (the root cause), then you'll likely end up right back where you were, repeating the same old pattern. This is why people attract the same abusive partners, end up in the same dismal jobs, and end up stressed, depressed, and hopeless.

Think of an inquisitive 4-year-old child who asks, "Why this?" or "Why that?" As adults, we find this endearing at first. After a while, all we hear is "Why?...Why?...Why?" The truth is that youngsters are innate problem solvers. Japanese manufacturers knew this and developed a problem-solving process called *The Five Whys*. The intent is to keep asking why until you identify the exact problem to solve. If you hear a clunking noise while driving your car, you don't start to fix random things. You take it to a mechanic in hopes of diagnosing the real problem. This is the same for you too. When you don't identify the *right* problem, then you'll likely waste time and resources, and often end up right back where you started. The Five Whys is proven successful in the business world, and it's a profoundly successful tool in your personal life too.

What to do: ask yourself five whys.

Any time you experience emotional pain, practice asking yourself why.

How to do it:

Ask yourself why in the following way:

"Why is it a problem to _____?" or,

"Why is it bad to _____?"

After you answer each question, delve deeper and ask another why question. When you ask enough why questions, you'll identify a limiting belief.

As you practice this exercise, you'll become keenly aware of the hyper-critical voice that tells you that you aren't good enough, successful, worthy, valuable, and so on. Sound familiar? Whether you believe it or not, these are thoughts that cause you the most suffering.

Break down your limiting beliefs.

Now that you have a limiting belief identified, inspect it and then break it down. Perhaps you've been navigating life thinking, "I won't be able to make ends meet doing what I love." The problem with this thought is that you don't know this for certain, do you? You don't know what will happen tomorrow, and you can't change what happened yesterday. You're basing your perception on a gap of uncertainty and letting your fears and worries dictate the outcome. This gap of uncertainty is the sweet spot; it's the space of *unlimited opportunity*.

World-renowned transformational leader Byron Katie teaches us to become curious about our thoughts by inspecting the truth of our reality through an inquiry tool she developed called *The Work*. In the process of using this tool, she's freed herself of a lifetime of suffering and has guided thousands of others to do the same.

Katie's theory is that when you believe an untrue story, you create suffering. The goal is to *accept your reality*. And, when you do, you free yourself from the pain you inflicted *on yourself* from believing false stories. Believing a set of false stories limits your perspective, and also limits your life.

What to do: inspect your thoughts.

As described in the exercise below, when you notice a limiting thought based on the results from your Five Whys, you'll inspect the reality of it and connect it with what you feel in your *physical body*. Then, you'll inspect the reality of an opposing statement that could also be true, or even truer than the original limiting thought. Most often, you'll realize that you've believed a false reality and will feel a great sense of inner peace once you've accepted the truth.

You can also take The Work a step further and connect the thought with your emotions and behaviors. This may help you identify triggers and patterns.

How to do it:

Write down the limiting thought and inspect it.

- Is it true?
- Is it absolutely true?
- How do you react when you believe the thought?
- Who would you be without the thought?
- Reconstruct the limiting thought into a sentence that has the opposite meaning, but nearly the same words.

- Write three examples of where this opposing thought is true in your recent past.

Inspecting your thoughts is a way of transforming your way of thinking. Turning around the thought to the opposite creates a new perspective and most often sheds light on your reality. Learn to inspect your thoughts, and you will be well on your way to freedom.

Finally, and most importantly, remember that you're in a continual state of metamorphosis. Trust that you will find the answers. Being stuck in the gap of uncertainty can feel quite terrifying. Be kind and patient with yourself as you get quiet, question everything, break down your limiting thoughts and shed your skin.

It's within the muck that the real magic happens! .

CHAPTER

Two

Surviving
By Amanda Lee

AMANDA LEE

Amanda Lee, previously known as Amanda Handke, was born in Colorado yet raised most of her childhood in Guttenberg and Sioux City, Iowa. She currently lives in the beautiful state of Colorado with her husband and two children. Amanda respects the arts; whether it is dancing in her home to Disney songs or attending musicals and art exhibits, she loves it all. When feeling inspired, she enjoys painting, songwriting and writing screenplays. Amanda loves hiking, coloring with her children, and playing Yahtzee with her family. You can reach Amanda at: leehealingmassage@gmail.com if you would like to get in touch with me. As I stated in my article, I am not qualified to be a counselor, but I might be able to lead you in the right direction.

Acknowledgments

I would like to honor my grandfather, Lloyd Biederman. He would constantly remind me never to give up on my dreams and to fight for what I believed in. He was the strong voice that guided me through my childhood and the positive affirmations that I tell myself today. I would like to thank my mother and sisters that saw me through this nightmare and loved me through all the hurt. I would like to thank my husband and children for being patient with me and allowing me the time I need to continue healing. Thank you to my editor, Ronnie Carroll, and As You Wish Publishing for helping my voice be heard and publishing my first article. I would also like to thank my readers; I hope you discover your courage and motivation from this article. Thank you all for being such a big part of my journey.

Surviving
By Amanda Lee

We've been put in a box of misfits, labeled "troubled, uneducated, sexual deviants" because of our abuse. We didn't choose this life, but it is something we live with every day. I choose to write now not because this is the best time in my life to do so, or because I'm feeling like I have succeeded at life or even because I feel like I could be a life coach for someone at this time. No, I am writing because I want to be part of a movement. I want to be the change and erase some of the stigmas and misbeliefs that we have told ourselves. I'm doing this to open the door to a brighter life, a brighter me, and a brighter tomorrow.

I want survivors to be able to carry this book as a reminder that you are not alone and to help steer you in the right direction to begin your healing process, although it is important to find a counselor and a group you can be a part of. This book will be here if you are feeling lost and don't know where to begin, like I once was.

It's here for you when you are waiting to hear back from the 50 therapists you called, and no one seems to call you back, or when the suicide hotline puts you on hold. It's here when you're waiting through the nights of flashbacks and feel like you are crazy, or when nothing seems to be helping and you have hit your wall. This book and my words will be here to remind you that you are not alone. You're never alone.

Unfortunately, one out of every four females and one out of every six males have reported sexual abuse. The numbers are astonishing, and I hope that soon more people will start speaking up. I hope we will have stronger voices for our children. This is something I cannot do alone; the more people who speak up, the more awareness there will be around this uncomfortable, awkward topic. Along with this awareness, I hope that the blame, the ugliness, and uncomfortable, awkward shame will shift from the survivor to the perpetrator. I hope that this allows many others to start their healing process and join me in being a survivor and no longer the victim.

My journey has many twists, blurred flashbacks, misunderstood emotions and pain, something you might relate to. It started with a deep-seated discomfort and knowing I shouldn't trust my father but not understanding fully why. Sure, he had his bad days where he got angry and risked our lives or verbally abused my sisters and me, but wasn't this all a normal part of being human? Doesn't everyone have an evil side? A lot of other people seemed to enjoy being around him, and we shared a lot of laughs. So, why? Why, did I feel so violated when around this man, my father, whom other girls adored and found safety and security within?

When I was twenty, I got a phone call from my sister who said something had happened and asked if I could come to get her. I was attending college 30 minutes away at the time and felt the need to go rescue her but, I went numb and couldn't get to her until the next day. She told me my father had touched her and she confirmed that what we experienced was more than mere nightmares like we had been told. She confirmed the anger, the pain, and our not knowing what to do with all the hell that was now our reality. In our childhood, we made a pinky-promise never to talk about our troubled past. We acknowledged that right now was finally the time to break that vow of silence. She was—and is—my fearless partner, forever friend, strong, powerful twin and the proof that the horror we had to live through was not something we made up or brought upon ourselves simply because we were twins and were forced to act out a man's twisted fantasies. We were not to blame but, at the time, neither of us understood that. My sister went on to seek help and to start her healing journey. As for me, I resorted to what I knew— disassociation. I proceeded to drown my nightmares with alcohol and cigarettes for many years.

About a year after we shared that conversation in the car, I got a call from my sister saying that Virgil (my father) was cheating on my mother. She asked if I could again come home and help with family matters. A week later, I moved home and proved that my father was cheating. My mother started her own investigation and began divorce proceedings. My sister talked me into attending massage school, and my competitive nature and curiosity forced me to apply. Although I didn't fully acknowledge who I was healing, massage school started the process for me.

Attending Bio-Chi Institute for Massage Therapy in Sioux City, Iowa changed my life and taught me my first healthy coping strategies. Throughout the program, I learned what it meant to be truly present. I had strength inside of me that no one could violate because I could control it. I reminded myself of how creative and intelligent I was. The only person that stands in your way as an adult is yourself. I taught myself to be accountable for my actions, and how to breathe and protect myself through Chi Gong. At the end of my massage program, I had healed my past and was ready to start my practice helping others heal. I had moved on, so I thought, and was ready to move forward.

Around age 26, I found myself in a dark place again. My flashbacks, constant at this time, had grown to be unbearable. I wanted to end my life not because I didn't want to live, but because I didn't know how to deal with the horrific flashbacks. I still didn't know how to define what was happening to me, and I questioned if I was making it all up. I wanted to be normal like everyone thought my family had been. After a long search, I found a counselor. Her name was Watson, and I became Sherlock Holmes, and together, we uncovered the mysteries of my past.

My father, who never wanted to reveal his secrets, instilled my belief that only the weak sought out counseling and talked about their feelings. But, through counseling, I finally was starting to feel human again, and the anxiety and pain inside me were not so intense. My therapist and I talked a lot about the Karpman's Drama Triangle, and grounding skills to remind myself yet again how to stay present. I began to realize that every relationship I had at that time was unhealthy. My family was angry with me for a while, not understanding what was going on because I wasn't going to be part of the triangle anymore. So, I slowly rebuilt my role in my family from being a victim to a survivor, and everyone eventually got used to the new me.

Around this time, I was introduced to "Wings Foundation," a group for adult survivors of childhood sexual abuse. My first group meeting was a blur, and I went home and sobbed. I was relieved I wasn't alone, and yet a part of me was hoping that my family was the only family this happened to so that others didn't have to endure that pain and confusion I still struggle with at times.

Soon after my healing process began, I met the man I married. He listened without judgment, attended "Wings Loved Ones Group" on his own, and stood by me through the emotional roller coaster we rode when I found out I was pregnant with our first daughter. My sister and husband drove me to Virgil's house so I could drop a letter in his mailbox. In the letter I told him I remembered what he did (I went into detail) and I told him never to have any contact with me again. I would no longer tolerate any contact when I had a family to protect. This was six years ago, and I've had no contact with him since. I say that with a little pain in my heart because I deserved to have the best father. My children are of the utmost importance to me, and I can't imagine anyone with children not feeling that way. Parenthood has been the most challenging, heartbreaking, debilitating, PTSD trigger for me. Yes, it is also beautiful, but I won't lie. As I write this, I am struggling with the fact that I cannot control everything in their lives. Seeing them experience an ounce of pain tears me apart and impairs my breathing. My children are my main reason for writing this. I want to create a better world, a safer world. My oldest child is now five years old and so the last couple of years have been somewhat triggering, as those are the ages, I remember the most clearly from my abuse. I was old enough to remember and young enough not to disassociate.

When I was pregnant with my second girl, I signed up with "Wings" to do "SpeakOut," something I'd been delaying to do until I was mentally healthier. The scariest, most empowering moment of my life at that time was the moment I shared out loud, on a stage, for everyone to hear, that my father molested me. A part of the grooming (brainwashing) process for me came with many threats that to this day can haunt me if I let it. When I shared my story, it felt as if a part of my pain leaped off that stage and left me forever. I continued to do public speaking events for a network out of Denver to raise awareness around sex trafficking. In addition to making the world a better place, it was an essential part of my healing process. My hope is that someone will read this article and will want me to share my story with them. I continue to hope I can help raise awareness and change the outcome for someone in my audience.

It was so important for me to define that I was indeed a victim of childhood sexual abuse and what I turned to repeatedly was written in the book, *The Courage to Heal* by Ellen Bass and Laura Davis. Reading this for the first time made me realize that even if my flashbacks were foggy, the clarity of my memories was justification enough to remove Virgil out of my life and confirm I was sexually abused by the man. This book validated my reality, and I started focusing on self-care, getting out of the triangle and moving forward because I was sick of feeling stuck.

The Karpman's Drama Triangle is a diagram I referred to when I was in an unhealthy conversation or thought process. It is recognizing if you are playing the role of a "Victim, Persecutor, Rescuer" or a combination of all three, the "Martyr." I recognize this dynamic when I find myself making decisions for someone, trying to rescue them. In this, I would become a victim because they were not returning the favor. I would start to feel sorry for myself and go down a rabbit hole of self-pity. Then I would get angry (the Persecutor) and yell at whomever was in the triangle with me, accusing that they should have helped and come to my rescue. So, the key to getting to a healthy thought process was to realize that I was in the triangle and needed to get out of it. In this scenario, I would remind myself that I am only in control of me and can't control how others react. I can only control my reactions. I would either apologize to the person or remove myself from the situation to give me time to process what I was feeling and why this was affecting me so much. I encourage the reader to look more into Karpman's Drama Triangle in the hope it adds another coping mechanism to your toolbox.

The meditation breathing that I was taught through the practice of Qi Gong is another coping mechanism that helped me. Along with reminding myself to be present by naming three things I could touch, see and hear, I would place my hand on my lower belly. As I would breathe in, I would imagine myself breathing in all the healthy energy while expanding my lower abdomen. Then as I exhaled, I would eliminate all the negative energy while relaxing my mind, body, and soul. I would repeat this whenever negative thoughts came into my mind until I was in a healthy place.

My intentions are pure, and I hope that you will find peace in the words I share. If you are feeling triggered by this article, please don't sit alone in your thoughts. Practice one of these exercises, go speak to a family member or friend or call a crisis hotline.

I have worked hard to be here today, and I will continue this fight. I say fight because for me it is a constant battle of reminding myself that I too have these skills and need to remember to use them. I hope that my article will help others continue their fight and go on to be the healthiest you possible. Please help me in creating this brighter future that I dream of.

CHAPTER

Three

Growth Out Of The Ashes
By Dr. Angela Marick

DR. ANGELA MARICK

Dr. Angela Marick is an inspirational speaker, writer, mindset coach, and owner of ShatterBox Coaching. Her life's mission is to massively empower people to grow through life's inevitable challenges as a life coach. She lives in York with her husband, Paul, their three sons, and two dogs. Her education includes a BS in Nutrition from Cornell University and a Doctor of Chiropractic degree from Palmer College of Chiropractic. After losing her first husband, Josh, she went on to write a book about her experience with grief. With her training, compassion, and experience of tragedy and personal transformation, Dr. Angela uplifts her audiences and clients with deep conversations about growth and possibility. You can contact her via:

Email: drangela@shatterboxcoaching,

Facebook: www.facebook.com/shatterboxmama/

Website: www.shatterboxcoaching.com, or purchase her book, *Beauty in the Brokenness: One Woman's Voice* at www.drangelamarick.com

Acknowledgments:

I want to express my gratitude to Paul, my rock and soul mate; Justin, Will and Carter, our incredible boys; Josh, my angel husband; my coaches, Troy Dukowitz, Stacey Smith; my parents; my team at White Rose Family Chiropractic; my faith that gets deeper through each challenge of life, and the countless beautiful souls that I have encountered along my journey in life.

Growth Out Of The Ashes
By Dr. Angela Marick

"Whether you think you can, or you think you can't, you're right."
—Henry Ford

Our thoughts literally create our reality. Sounds so simple, right? Until we genuinely work to believe it. I mean deeply believe it to our core. I have spent so much of my life in mind-drama about all the reasons why I'm not enough which I can't get out of my head. It was only an excuse not to become who I wanted to be. I was living a lie. I was living the lie that I was repeatedly telling myself that I wasn't enough. I would spin in my mind and work to produce, almost like I was punishing myself. This is how I started my first business in 2010 as a chiropractor. I had the thought that if I work super hard and constantly take action, I'll be successful. So…I did. I ran around, worked super hard, took lots of action and managed success and growth in my business. What I didn't understand was that I was operating from a "not enough" premise. I had set out to prove something to myself, to my family, to my peers. Not from a place of true self-worth and self-belief.

I operated this way for years until 2015, when my husband, Josh, was diagnosed with an extremely rare, extremely aggressive form of cancer. The thoughts and beliefs I had operated in my life got upended immediately. I didn't know how to think about his cancer other than not to think about him dying. I decided to push that thought to the back of my mind. I moved forward, kept taking action and prayed for his healing. I did not let myself think about whether he would live or not. My whole adult life had revolved around my love for this man. My marriage to him had defined me, had defined my purpose in life, had been one of the main pillars of my existence. What do you mean he has cancer? You get married and then grow old together. Getting cancer at 39? What?

Josh made a decision when he was diagnosed. He chose to engage in life and live for whatever stretch of time he was allotted. He didn't spin in self-pity. He didn't spin in "Why me?" He unequivocally decided to live. He decided to create healthier habits. He decided to go to bed earlier, go on additional family trips, turn the computer off regularly, eat better and appreciate life by being present. He decided from his mind. He decided that he was going to live in the present. We have 60,000 thoughts per day and 47 percent focus on the future and the past—not the present. How can we engage in life completely if we focus on the future and past? How can you honestly hear what your teenager is telling you if you are distracted by work or by what someone said to you that made you angry? How can you serve that teenager who is in a season in his life where he is trying to figure out how to make decisions when you are "checked-out"?

May 11, 2016, marked the day of Josh's last breath. He left this life on his terms. He left with peace and completion of being present with the most important people in his life: me, our two boys (then 8 and 11), his parents and brother. We said goodbye in a magnificently beautiful way. I didn't consciously know this at the time, but I fully accepted his departure. I missed him like crazy and felt the bereaving acutely every day. But, this was my new reality. I now had a choice. I could choose to live in victimhood, a place where I blamed God and anything else that I could for the death of my love. Or, I could accept what occurred and relearn how to live in my new reality.

The thoughts that we attach to each circumstance create our feelings, create our actions, and finally, our results. I could have chosen to sit there. Instead, I started my healing process by caring for my mind and heart by working with people that would help me grow through this chapter of my life. I was beautifully surrounded by a great therapist, my life coach, dear friends and, my beloved family.

As I accepted my new reality, I manifested a new love in my life whom I met three months after Josh's passing. My thoughts quickly became consumed with self-judgment and anxiety. If I loved Josh, how could I love someone else so soon? As if my heart was finite and the love that it contained had a defined limit. To my huge surprise, it didn't have a limit. As I fell in love with this new man, Paul, I continued to raise my children, run my business and heal from the loss of Josh. I became acutely aware of all the thoughts that ran through my head. So many of them! So many that weren't serving the woman I was growing into. I had endured the most emotionally traumatic episode of my life, and I was still standing. I was finding meaning in this. This new man brought a whole new world to my life and a year after we met, we wed. Again, my continued self-judgment, as well as my perceived judgment from others, persisted. How could I move on so quickly? Am I doing the right thing? Can I not be alone? As I started to unpack these thoughts, I realized that there was nothing wrong with me. I had decided to partner with a new person and raise all three of our kiddos together in life. He honored my past, he engaged with me in my present and held space for my future.

My story is profound to me because of the meaning that I discovered, allowing me to realize that the beliefs we have can be transitory. They are our repeated thoughts. The way we perceive something is the lens that we choose to look at life. We can choose to change the lens and the focus. I chose to find beauty in the brokenness and to grow. One of the most pivotal supports I received during this time was from my life coach, Dr. Troy Dukowitz. I hired him in 2009. He held the space for me that I needed as I started and grew a business, as I supported my husband through his work, and as I raised our children. He held the space for me through the diagnosis, the death, the healing, the dating, the writing of my book, and finally, my transition into becoming a life coach. Years ago, I had no intention of being a coach. However, as Josh and I went through our massive life shift, I uncovered a passion and belief in myself to massively hold space for others in a way that allowed them to uncover their light—the light that they kept hidden because of un-serving thoughts. If you have 60,000 thoughts per day, how many serve you? I do a "thought download" every morning to check in and see where my mind is. Thought downloads can fill a page or two or three or more! Do you know your thoughts? How can we get the results we want in life if we don't know what we're thinking?

Grab your trusted journal and let's explore your mind.

1. What are all my thoughts? Examples: "I'm so tired." "This exercise is going to take too long." "I don't have enough time."

2. As you look at your thoughts, which is the one you are struggling the most with today?

3. As you think this thought, how do you feel

4. When you feel that way, how do you show up? What actions do you take or don't take?

5. And finally, what happens? What is the result of your actions?

6. Which is the result of the thought and feeling? If the results you are getting in life aren't serving your highest self or align with where you want to be, then the thoughts need to change. Let's work backward.

7. What result do you want? (Example: lose ten pounds or create five new clients for my business.)

8. Imagine what it feels like with that result. How would you look like 10 pounds lighter? How would your clothes feel? How empowered would you feel in your body? Or – if you were a life coach that signed 5 additional clients, what would your day look like? How would you be showing up for the day? How would you be feeling about your empowerment as a coach?

9. Sit in the space of the result. Think about it as if it is happening right now. What actions are you taking? What actions are you not taking because they don't serve this result? How do you feel in your body as this result becomes reality? What thoughts do you have?

Do you feel the difference? You get to choose the result you want and then sit with it often and choose it repeatedly until you resonate with it. I have struggled with this because I have the thought, but I still can't believe in myself. I am struggling with it even today. Then I remind myself of all the areas where I chose to think differently. I chose to believe differently, and I watched my life get better. I chose to stop believing the judgments of others, or more accurately, my perception of their judgments (which translated to me judging me). When I took the time to release them, I felt peace. I felt joy and love for myself, for my husband, for my children, for my peers, for my friends, for my world. When

I changed my thinking to serve who I am, I began to feel love for me, and it radiated and spilled into all areas of my life.

Are you struggling with where you are in life? Are you struggling with thoughts of self-belief or lack thereof? What do you deeply want right now? Take a moment. Take a breath. Or two or three. Put your hand over your heart and ask, "What do I genuinely want?" Sit and listen. Be patient. If you rush, you'll miss the message, telling your mind that you are too busy, and don't have time, because what you want isn't important enough. Stop it…and listen. Now that you got it, or at least the whisper of it, ask yourself, "Who do I need to be for this to become my reality? How do I feel when I step into this result? How does my life look different? What kind of woman am I?"

Have you ever done a ropes course? Even if you haven't, bear with me. As you cling to what you know or the place where you feel safe, the idea of letting go to grab the next level can be terrifying. However, when you gather the belief in yourself to take action to get to the next level, you rise up. Suddenly, you are seeing the world from a new view because you grew your consciousness.

As I left the place I knew—my life with Josh where I felt very secure and stable—I found a whole new world with new ideas and perceptions. Now that I'm a life coach, I see endless possibilities to serve my clients and to impact this world, and I am barely scratching the surface. As I commit to doing daily mindset work and taking the time to think deeply about each of my clients as well as the ones I will attract, I feel my results as if they are happening now. I am constantly going to that place to open up my consciousness of self-belief in this new level of results. The view gets clearer. Can you see it? Can you imagine it in your unique world? Be patient, give yourself grace and compare yourself to no one. This is your timing. This is your desire to impact the world on whatever platform or niche that reflects who you are.

You always have a choice. You always get to choose which path you want to take, even when it may seem unclear. Be mindful of your mind. It is amazing, and as you start to understand it more deeply and believe, you'll grow in your ability to manifest amazing results in your life. Get yourself a coach that will stand for your best version, hold you accountable, challenge you and support you like crazy from a place of love. Having support in my life was monumental in my ability to find powerful meaning and the courage to step forward into a completely new life. It was scary at times and overwhelming. I am now a life coach. I am now a mama to three boys and three dogs. I have an amazing husband who deeply supports and loves me and who I am completely in love with. I have this amazing life with no regrets. I have the incredible memories of Josh, who I shared so much life within our 20 years together.

How do you want your life to be? How do you want to show up for your life? For this world? Are you ready to let go of the vice grip of the obstacle thoughts that hold you back? They aren't serving you anymore. They aren't serving the version of you who is ready to show up as her authentic self in this world. You have something to say. You have something to offer. Why are you holding her back? Why are you silencing her? Are you ready to boldly step forward and create the life that you have an inkling of in your mind? Nurture that seed with pause, with thought work, with growing self-belief, and watch the magic happen!

CHAPTER

Four

One Common Thread: How You Are Already Living "On Purpose" By Cecilia Deal

CECILIA DEAL

Cecilia Deal is a bestselling Author, Speaker and Certified Career and Business Coach. She has successfully navigated career transitions and helped multiple organizations gain clarity about their purpose and vision. She helps individuals and small businesses clarify their purpose and message so they can communicate effectively and integrate their mission into their work or business. This allows her clients to make decisions that are more informed, create a path for growth and transition, and allows their work to become the vehicle in which they fulfill their purpose in life. You can reach her at cecilia@findingwanna.com or by visiting her website at www.findingwanna.com.

Acknowledgments

I'd like to thank my father who passed away many years ago but taught me strength, resilience, integrity and that people matter. I will be forever grateful for him. To my family who taught me so much and continue to support me, to my friends who were there to listen to me talk about the concepts contained in this article and its many versions and especially to God/universe/the divine, my deep appreciation for continuously showing me that I will always be supported and that we always get what we need from life.

One Common Thread: How You Are Already Living "On Purpose" By Cecilia Deal

"Your gift will always feel easy, simple and uncomplicated."
~ Cecilia Deal

I changed jobs every nine months or so early in my career, for the simplest reasons. My boss would change and I no longer felt in alignment with him, or the work was too easy and I no longer felt challenged, or I'd get bored and want a change.

After so many changes I had to start getting creative with how I presented myself on my resume and in interviews. How do you apply for a recruiting job when your last position was a database administrator? All the hiring manager would see was that I didn't have the experience to do the job.

So, I started reviewing my resume and looking for similarities in my work. From the Project Manager to the Recruiter, the Database Administrator to the Process Developer, from the healthcare field to banking, from Human Resource Consultant to Career Coach, how were they the same? What words could I use to explain their similarities, that they required the same skill set, and that I was passionate about all of it, even if the job title changed?

As I looked at my work history, I found similarities. I was a liaison in all positions working with different levels of management. I was frequently called to get in front of people and present, whether it was a project outline, computer training, or a new idea. I helped the leaders identify what they were really asking for, and I translated those ideas into workable projects and action items.

Then, I looked at the things I did that were not in my job description; like the fact that everyone came into my office to talk to me about how they wanted to change jobs or careers, or to ask about how they could communicate better with their co-workers or their spouses. This coaching wasn't part of my job, but these co-workers, executives and leaders found their way to my office anyway.

Friends would always reach out to speak to me about their goals, their excitement, their passion, to gain clarity about their interests, or what they wanted to achieve next in their work or careers. They would call me to gain clarity about the business they wanted to pursue, or the business decisions to make next that would set them on the right course and be right for them and their business.

As I looked at my personal life, I saw that friends would reach out to speak to me about their career and relationship goals. They wanted help understanding what it was they wanted from life. They wanted clarity about their interests and what they wanted to achieve next in their careers. They wanted to know what business to start, or what decisions to make that would set them off on the right course.

The more I looked, the more I saw similarities and patterns in what I did. I was a liaison, bridging the gap between where they were and where they wanted to be, and helping them find purpose and a mission. Working with them to clarify their vision, identify their needs and desires, unify their objectives, communicate more effectively, and finally put a plan in place to accomplish it.

I did this whether I was a Recruiter, Project Manager, Process Developer, Human Resource Consultant, Business Consultant or Career Coach. I did it in my personal life and in my work life, with friends, family, co-workers and strangers. In fact, I couldn't stop myself.

I realized that if I looked over the course of my life, I could see the same legacy running through everything. But, it wasn't just a legacy, it was a passion, my motivation, and my personal mission in life.

Then I started looking at the careers and experiences of those around me, and I saw patterns, similarities and themes in their lives too. Their own version of it, their purpose, personal mission, passion, their calling.

One common thread

There is a common thread lurking in your life too that ties everything together. Answering the questions "What am I passionate about? What is my purpose? What is my calling? What is it I am here in this life to do?"

You weave this thread - this theme - no matter where you are or what you do. Whether you work for someone else, yourself, or in multiple businesses and pursuits, whether you've held the same job or frequently switched careers, it weaves through every facet of your life. It runs through your personal relationships, your hobbies, and your home life.

What's wild to think about is that everyone around you is aware of it, except you. It is something people recognize in you and respond to. You are just too close to it to see it yourself.

This passion is something that happens naturally, without you thinking about it. People come to you for help with it, whether it's part of your job description or not. And, you use all your talents and gifts to help.

It's something you excel at and take for granted. You think everyone should be able to do what you do because it comes easily to you. You wonder why others can't do it, even get angry when they don't. You think "Why would it not come easy to everyone else if it is so easy for you?"

You get caught up in it without thinking of it as a chore. You lose time when you are doing it; you may even forget to stop and eat. You hardly notice time passing. It always brings you great joy in the doing of it, and tremendous satisfaction when you're done.

Most likely, it is something you've never even thought of and you miss it every time. And, if you are like me, you keep running around asking other people "What am I good at? What is my passion? What is it I am here to do?" They can't put their finger on it either. But, if you told them – if you knew the words to describe it – they'd say, "of course!"

This one common thread is what you're talented at, it's your gift! It is what you carry with you regardless of what you are doing or who you are helping. This is your *calling*!

So what is that?

Is it like Lisa who changed careers from IT management to biology, but still carried the same passion, drive, gifts, motivations, and talents. She wouldn't have thought that IT and biology had anything in common, but it does. Both positions require the ability to problem solve, or follow protocol to find a solution or an answer, whether in research or a computer program.

Or is it like Mary who owned three different businesses and felt like somehow she was three different people, until she realized that her purpose, her passion and her drive were the same in every case. She was called to bring joy, power, and freedom to her clients as they faced and emerged from challenging life transitions. She realized that each business offered assistance in a different capacity and worked at a different step in the process for her clients who were at a slightly different stage in the game. Figuring out that she was the same person for each business, driven from the same underlying purpose and direction, she finally felt whole and complete instead of separated and disconnected.

Or is it like me, switching careers multiple times throughout my life, but finally seeing that they were all essentially the same? I was helping people gain clarity around their purpose, talents, and vision, and being the liaison to bridge that gap in understanding. I was helping them communicate clearly, unify their vision for life, and then put a plan in place to get where they wanted to go. I finally realized that while I held different roles (Recruiter, Database Administrator, Project Manager, and Coach), I was still working in a similar capacity each time, just with a different job title, a different business, on a different platform.

Once you understand what your one common thread is and you have a solid grasp on your talents and gifts, you can move into anything. *Anything!* Because you will know what you're passionate about, you will know how and whom to serve. Then *you* can choose the capacity in which you serve, and fulfill your personal mission in life, instead of having that decision made for you.

You'll feel whole and complete, as if your entire life finally makes sense, and that maybe you haven't been wasting your time at your current job, business, or relationship.

Then you can decide. "Do I want to stay where I'm at or do I want to put my efforts into a new direction?" At the very least you can know that your whole career, business pursuits and relationships all had a purpose, a reason, and a common link. You've been following your passion to fulfill your mission in life. It really has been all worthwhile.

What is your one common thread?

I start helping my clients find it by asking:

- What job did you have in high school that you loved? What were you doing? What were your day-to-day activities? What did you do that was not in your job description?

- What is, or has been, the best job in your career? What was required of you, what did you volunteer to do?

- What was the worst job you have had in your career? What did you try to avoid? What did you do instead? What got you into trouble? Where did you spend most of your time?

- What volunteer work do you do? How do you contribute to your community?

- What do you do for extracurricular activities? What groups are you involved in? What do you always seem to volunteer to do? What do you always get asked to do?

- What did your friends come to you for – advice, directions, lessons, or something else?

"But Cecilia, I don't have a passion or purpose, you say. "There isn't one thing I'm really good at. How do I figure this out?"

That's funny! Because realistically, you have been doing what you are passionate about your whole life. You may not think of it as something you can consider a passion. In fact, you may not have thought of it at all. But you have been doing it your whole life and have woven it into everything you do. It is who you are, at a very essential level. Because it is so much of who you are, you don't think much of it at all.

Throughout my life, co-workers would end up in my office to talk about their careers. Friends would reach out to gain clarity about their interests and their passions. Complete strangers would start telling me their life stories. It just took some time for me to realize that they saw in me what I couldn't see – that my purpose in life had always been a part of me.

Many years ago, a client of mine who worked as an engineer, thought engineering was all he was good at. We talked through all his job transitions and each one was the same. When I dove deeper, asking what extracurricular activities he enjoyed with his co-workers and how he interacted with them, he told me he was always the "class clown" lightening the mood and making everyone laugh. It always made getting through the tough times easier. My client later explained that he had a side job as a clown, and he loved it! He had built a whole business around it. It gave him the joy that a person finds when they follow their passion.

So guess what his passion was?

By making people laugh, lightening the mood, and helping people get through the hard times, he followed his passion. He loved sharing his talents, and especially loved helping others who really needed him. He did this all the time, at his engineering job, as his side job, with family and friends. He wove it through every facet of his life.

In truth, you are meant to do what you are passionate about doing. Put a name to it, get some clarity around it, and start making choices in life with it as your personal compass. You will feel more fulfilled, more satisfied, and more alive. Your life has meaning. Find it and live it.

CHAPTER

Five

What Story Are You Telling Yourself
By Demi Stevens

DEMI STEVENS

Dr. Demi Stevens, CEO, Year of the Book press, turns writing dreams into successfully published books. She has personally assisted in the production of 300 titles by more than 125 authors, ranging from children's picture books to sizzling romance, award-winning mysteries, and bestselling business books.

She holds degrees from West Virginia University, Capital, Northwestern, and Ohio State, and has served on the faculties of

Ohio State and Delaware Valley University, and as Director of Paul Smith Library.

Many writers call Demi the "Book Whisperer," but perhaps "Book Midwife" is more appropriate, because literary labor and delivery can be so painful. Each year she coaches a limited number of writers one-on-one through the entire drafting, editing, and publishing process. To learn more, visit: YOTBpress.com

Acknowledgments

Thanks to my husband, Todd, for believing in me before I believed in myself.

What Story Are You Telling Yourself
By Demi Stevens

Do you realize that 81 percent of Americans want to write a book before they die? Most households can't even get 81 percent agreement on what to have for dinner!

Possibly you're letting a life story or book idea of your own simmer... waiting for the illusive "Someday" when the kids are grown, retirement checks roll in, laundry is folded, and all eight planets align (unless Pluto gets re-admitted, then it will take an extra thousand years).

You know this is illogical, but at the end of the day you're exhausted. It's easier to grab the remote than a pen. Your stacks of gorgeous journals lay untouched on a bookcase somewhere. You may be intellectually ready to channel your inner James Patterson or Nora Roberts, but your outer channel is locked on Netflix.

And when you do wake in the middle of the night with an incredible idea (because the Muse keeps odd hours), it's forgotten before the coffee brews.

Here's the thing, If you keep waiting for the "right" time, you will only find what's "left." And what's left is, nothing, because whatever time you aren't using for yourself, someone else is going to fill with needs from their agenda.

Where You Place Your Attention is Where You'll See Results

It's no mystery that if you plant seeds in the spring, and keep them watered and weeded, they will bear fruit (or vegetables, or flowers) later in the year. But everything worth harvesting requires care and attention. We might wish we could birth our children and then ignore them for eighteen years and they'd still turn out okay, but… really?

My hope for you today is that you'll find the inspiration and motivation and *courage* to move forward toward your dream of writing a book. The mysterious aura that surrounds writing is just leftover pollution from those '80s writers who chain-smoked their way to The End. Let's demystify the process and get you started.

What Does Progress Look Like?

If you've ever cleaned out your bedroom closet, or attic, or garage, then you already understand that in order to make progress, things have to get messy. Yet there can be order within the chaos.

Since there are no book police traveling door to door, you can begin any way you like, but I'm going to outline a method here that I've used one-on-one with hundreds of people just like you (aka folks who never wrote a book before, but had a burning idea, combined with some doubt and hesitation). You can use this process to get your book idea out of your brain and down onto paper or the computer—and not just start to write, but actually complete your whole draft.

What you do with your book after that is up to you. One 86-year-old author friend keeps his memoir in a spiral-bound note-book for his adult children to find after he passes. Other folks print enough copies to hand out to family members at the holidays. But most consider publishing so they can share their stories with the larger world. I've helped authors navigate all these methods, including indie publishing through my Year of the Book press. There are a world of choices available to you, but the first step is always the same.

You've gotta write the book!

Perfection is a Form of Procrastination

The "Someday" dream is a smaller symptom of a much larger disease. It affects you not only as a writer, but as a friend, co-worker, parent, and human being. When you limit yourself to only sharing your "best" work, you neglect to realize that you don't have to share the "draft" work.

The first promise I need you to make is to release your draft writing from the evil claws of perfectionism. I don't care what mystic you're channeling, there will be typos and the need for an editor before we're done. But that time is *not now*.

Now is the time for scribbles, brainstorming, raw and passionate ideas, and for absolutely schlocky ideas, too. I need you to crawl out to the edge of the limb and look around where you can see things differently. You don't have to let go of the branch… just keep your eyes and mind open to possibilities.

Step One: I'd like you to fire up your word processor or grab a pen and some blank paper. (But remember: we're not being perfectionists. If all you have at hand is the back of an envelope and a crayon, that'll work, too.)

On this page, I'd like you to toss out ideas of what your book is about. Just scrawl them down. It doesn't have to be complete sentences. Spelling does not count. There are no wrong answers. There are only ideas.

Please, please, please *do not dismiss any thoughts that flow to you.* Can you imagine how awful it would feel to be part of a brainstorming group where the leader won't write your idea on the whiteboard? Promise me you will treat your Muse with more respect. We'll be picky later, but right now it's far more important to honor your creativity!

Set a Timer

Have you ever noticed that tasks take the full amount of time you have to offer?

If a term paper were due in three weeks, how many classmates would turn theirs in on Day Two? And how many would write their entire paper the final evening? So then it could've been done in just a single day, right? Because, in fact, it was. It simply "needed" those previous 20 days of annoying dread and whining in order to properly ferment.

So let's get one more thing straight: if you can devote 15 minutes a day, most days each week—without going back to correct the early material before you've drafted all the way to The End—then you can truly reach your dream goal of writing your book in the next six months.

The secret is in saying "No" to procrastination. Just like perfectionism, it is not your friend. In fact, it's the older brother who'll try to drown you in the bathtub the first time you're not looking. Do not give in to the sabotage!

3 Minutes: "On Your Mark..."

If you're still waiting for the "right" time to tackle *Step One*, that time is *now.* I want you to get ready to write, and set a timer for *only 3 minutes.* This is all you'll need once you understand how to do this.

Your job during all your writing sessions is to get your fingers typing or your pen moving—as soon as the timer starts. I don't care if all you write is "I hate Demi for making me do this." Your brain will soon discover what a colossal waste of time that is, and will supply you with something much worthier.

You also must allow yourself never to cross anything out during this drafting process. Stop fussing with the backspace key. Your first draft is all about *creating*. This process of *creation* does not need *deletion*. Save that for an editing day. A long time from now.

I also want you to release yourself from caring about proper spelling or punctuation or grammar. No one should be grading this draft, least of all you!

If you find yourself pausing to look for the "perfect" word, I want you to draw a blank line and keep going with the rest of your thought. After the timer goes off, you can go back and do a read-through later. Almost always, that missing word will pop into your brain instantly, without wasting precious "date time" with your Muse.

"Get Set…"

In the box below, or on your own computer or paper, it's time to begin answering the question: "What's Your Book About?"

Consider things like genre (cookbook, how-to, memoir, romance, science fiction), the characters or topics included (who or what you will write about), and the scope of the book (how much time it spans or how many recipes or techniques it includes).

Write as much as you can in these 3 minutes. Remember, there are no wrong answers.

"...Go!"

The Power of 15 Words

Now that you've got *a lot of words* about your book, I want you to focus on just a few that sum it all up. This process will also become one of your best teachers about writing craft. Mark Twain used to say, "I apologize for such a long letter—I didn't have time to write a short one."

When you value your readers' time by saying things elegantly and succinctly (aka short and sweet), they'll find your book virtually irresistible.

Imagine someone asks you what your book is about. You stumble and stutter, say a lot about a little, and ultimately not much. What if instead you could tell them:

What happens to a vampire after he finally dies? Heaven? Hell? Nope, purgatory in a West Hollywood warehouse. Go figure. ["Cold in California," by Deb Riley-Magnus]

Now it's time to mold those loose thoughts into a single line that grabs attention, and won't make someone's eyes glaze over.

3 More Minutes

Got your book pitch done? Now it's time to put away the first assignment and move on.

Step Two: Using a fresh 3-minute timer, I want you to make a bullet-point list of scenes or topics that should be covered in your book.

If you're writing a cookbook, list the recipes. If a memoir is your focus, jot down critical moments that have to be included. For a business book, list all the topics that make up your chapters.

The same rules apply: start writing immediately, don't cross anything out (no backspace/delete key), and keep writing the entire time ("I hate Demi" if you have to).

The Power of 15 Minutes

Step 3 and last step: Is one you'll do over and over from now until The End.

I want you to visit your list of scenes and choose one. It doesn't matter if you write out of order. It only matters that you write.

Set your timer for 15 minutes for each session, and remind yourself there is no one else who can tell this story but you. Do not to worry about style or flair. That's a task of revision. Later. Your job right now, is to *write now*.

Focus on that topic or scene and let the words pour out of you for the full 15 minutes. Keep scribbling. Keep typing. Don't press backspace. Don't click delete. Do not pass "Go" and perhaps you'll one day collect "$200." (Hopefully more.)

Remember that no one but you is going to see this draft. Spelling doesn't count any more than it would if your six-year-old son wrote you a "luv ltr." Grammar is a luxury, not a requirement. If your sentences tend to run on, buy them sneakers.

If you need to write dialogue, just get the words down. All the quotation marks are icing on the word-cake later. Most anyone could fill those in for you, but *only you* can write your story.

And finally, I need you to promise me you're not going to waste time going back and re-reading each scene after you write it. Or at least, if you can't stop yourself, then pinkie-swear you won't start editing until after you've got a draft of every single scene.

I can't tell you the number of first-time writers who draft Chapter 2, only to have an "epiphany" about Chapter 1. So they go back and "correct" the opening before doing anything else. If they're lucky, they move on to Chapter 3, but, I'll be darned, they have another "epiphany." This cycle of writing and re-writing continues *ad nauseam*. At a certain point, the joy of writing goes out a tall window, often followed by the laptop.

Revising your Chapter 1 is like buying an expensive pair of prescription glasses, when tomorrow you're going in for cataract surgery.

You need to write all the way through your draft so you can figure out what's truly important. When you have a moment of insight, just make a note inside the chapter where you discovered it. Maybe that fourth epiphany is going to get murdered by the fifth. Thank goodness you didn't lose time chasing a red herring.

Now it's your turn again. Select your first scene or topic, set your 15-minute timer, and write with joy! It's the best 15 minutes you'll have each day. And if 15 turns into 30 or more, you can thank me later.

Fear is a 4-Letter Word

As you begin your daily writing practice, you'll experience a variety of emotions... including *resistance*—the head trash that keeps you from starting. Sometimes the voice says: "I can't do this," or "I'm not good enough." Other times it's crueler: "You suck," "You're stupid," or "No one's ever gonna read this."

It's important to note these are all the voice of fear. Every single writer on the planet—whether a "nobody," "celebrity," or seasoned *NY Times* bestseller—hears these voices each time they approach a new project.

Yes, your favorite author in the world gets scared, too. It's known as Imposter Syndrome, and no one is immune.

"I have written 11 books, but each time I think, 'Uh oh, they're going to find out now. I've run a game on everybody, and they're going to find me out'." — *Maya Angelou*

With a little stick-to-it-iveness, you can win this battle, too. Writers are a courageous tribe, but don't mistake *courage* for *fearlessness*. Courage is merely taking action in spite of fear. You can write even though the voices try to warn you away. And when you do, your true voice will find its strength… and soon it will drown out the head trash.

At least for a time.

Because writing important truths makes us vulnerable. If you're scared of sharing your story, that's a signal! You've just located what you were set on earth to teach. It's time to be brave so others can see your light to guide their way.

What Would You Try If You Knew You Could Not Fail?

It's your time. Time to believe in yourself as much as I believe in you. The world needs your story. Today is your "Someday." Make this your Year of the Book.

CHAPTER

Six

Put Me In, Coach
By Dina F. Gilmore

DINA F. GILMORE

Dina F. Gilmore (aka She Who Heals Plenty or Ashwani) is a certified Shamanic Practitioner, Spiritual Mentor and Coach, Licensed Massage Therapist, Reiki Master Teacher, Photographer, Filmmaker, Scriptwriter, Podcaster and multiple bestselling author of "When I Rise, I Thrive" and "Healer." Gilmore is a southerner who grew up in Texas, then moved to Colorado in 2012 to thrive in a diverse state and build community connections. Coaching became a norm, so she created Mobile Shaman to mentor, share the healing art of Shamanism across the country in our modern-day society, and guide individuals toward creating their lives with purposeful action. Gilmore leads Shamanic Journey Circles, teaches various healing classes, is currently pursuing her degree in Digital Media Journalism, and is President of Rocky Mountain Media found on Anchor.fm, iTunes, Spotify and Google Podcasts.

shewhohealsplenty.wixsite.com/mobileshaman
shewhohealsplenty@gmail.com
www.facebook.com/MobileShaman-1223497391116026/
anchor.fm/rocky-mountain-media

Acknowledgments

I offer my deepest gratitude for the multitude of coaches I have had in my life. I love you dearly for your time and energy you've put into impacting and empowering my journeys. Thank you to my compassionate and beautiful momma, Bonnie. You will always be my biggest and greatest supporter. Thank you to Renee McGee for being my best friend. Colorado would not have been possible without you. Thank you also to Kathy C., Lyn Birmingham, Bhola Banstola, Spirit Moon Community, Chuck Murphy, Elizabeth Harbin, Dana "Spirit Butterfly" Parker, Kyra Schaefer, Helen Cook, Dot, Gerry Hollingshead, and Landmark Education for all the coaching and teachings. Special thanks to my tribe: Jeannie Church, Jeanne Sajonas, Ash Owen, and Maria Sison-Wright. Loving support and thanks to Dawn Lewis and Vicki Vehanen, my SMRT family.

Put Me In, Coach
By Dina F. Gilmore

In life, there are many types of coaches. I played sports during my entire childhood, so I learned quickly how my coaches' feedback improved my game and performances. Little did I know that, as an adolescent, sports would parlay into a real-life experience in choosing to be on the field in my personal and professional life. As I reflect, I chose to sit on the bench because I thought it would be easier, less mess, or spare me disappointment. Thankfully, I decided to get my butt off the sidelines and put myself in the game. Win or lose, it was essential for me to choose to act versus react to my surroundings or what I perceived was happening to me based on my past. Like any game, I encountered several obstacles to overcome in my life that was instrumental in shaping the woman I am now.

I found extraordinary courage after I met a new co-worker who was openly gay and attending college. She was living the life I wanted for myself. Her freedom of self-expression was inspiring, and I generated the nerve to tell one friend that I was gay. While I lost that friendship, it did not stop me from wanting to break free from the shackles and chains of my upbringing. I gained the courage to tell my momma, and at first, it went well. However, her friends, our family, and our Southern Baptist church had strong opinions and judgments that greatly influenced Momma's actions. Momma and I had a terrible fight that ended with a suitcase of my clothes thrown on the lawn. I was heartbroken, homeless, and terrified. My decisions were always made for me growing up, so I felt lost. I was a homeless gay teen statistic, but the alternative of being forced to attend Conversion Therapy was worth every night I slept in the bed of my truck.

Being gay is not a choice or lifestyle that you can force someone into converting. I was finally free to be me, and there was no going back. I am grateful for my Southern roots that built my foundation and birthed great determination to strive in becoming the best version of me. Thankfully, Momma and I have healed tremendously from the past and are closer than ever. She had to halt the stories and opinions being projected onto her. Momma chose to make the conscious decision of reconnecting with me and is now my biggest supporter. She took actions based on the love for her daughter, disregarding what family and congregation members were saying. Momma stood in her power and used her voice. I am grateful to this loving shift that healed and mended our past when many others in my LGBTQ (Lesbian, Gay, Bisexual, Transgender, Questioning) community are not as fortunate.

Life is what happens around you when you sit on the bench instead of actively participate in creating what you want your life to look like. I spent too many years trying to be what everyone else wanted me to be instead of becoming what or who I wanted to be in the world. I allowed my past to dictate my life because I listened to other people's expectations of me. This is the biggest injustice you can do to yourself. The words "I was not good enough, there is too much competition and that I will never make it" became my false truth. I dropped out of college in 1991 because I buckled to those hurtful words and it felt too overwhelming. Succumbing to the hate, I attempted suicide after I had "come out" as gay. I always knew I was gay, but I was terrified to live as the real me, and a drastic mistake turned into an empowering purpose. This all happened in four years. I chose to write my chapter for you, be vulnerable, and share in a way that empowers your actions toward the greatness you are destined to be and become. I believe in you. Will you join me and believe in yourself?

You can accomplish anything you set your mind toward—intentions and actions taken to achieve personal or professional goals. Determination and perseverance are important components to unlock or overcome any challenges you may face. Here are some helpful questions to assist on your journey of self.

- Am I living my life for me?

- What are my biggest dreams?

- Am I allowing anyone else to decide my future, or goals I wish to accomplish?

- Do I have any regrets that I want to change, revisit, or are holding me back?

- Am I doing what I love or am passionate about?

No matter what your answers were, congratulations on uncovering something new for yourself. You can consciously choose to take a new action. Fear may always be present, so acknowledge it. How you act versus react in your life profoundly impacts your journey. Fear is False Evidence Appearing Real and frequently has a story attached to it. Some of the best guidance I can offer you is never to let anyone tell you that you cannot do something. This is your life. You are the artist in charge of creating the masterpiece that is divinely you. A helpful tip is to give yourself room to get messy, heal, grow, be gentle with yourself, and turn your mistakes into learning opportunities for what works and does not work for you. You have the choice and freedom to decide. That is the beauty of being a human being. You can either be your worst enemy or your best cheerleader. You deserve to be celebrated and to put yourself first. Your relationship with yourself is the most important one, and many times, we lose sight of that.

In April 2014, at the age of forty-five, I attended a weekend Landmark forum on transformational work that would ultimately resolve my past and provide new ways of being to return to my childhood dreams. That one weekend was instrumental in rebirthing my authentic self. I could take new actions in the face of fear, separate from my past. This was the exact coaching I desperately craved to inspire me to get back in the game of my life and stop watching from the sidelines. While I am grateful for my twenty-year career in massage therapy and being a healer for myself and others, something deeper was missing. The body represents a piece of clay to me, ready to be molded and sculpted, but a grander impact was lacking. Pursuing my original art dreams brought me back to life—the life I always envisioned. Landmark methodology provided ultimate freedom from my past being rooted in my identity of being gay with old beliefs buried in expectations, judgments, and limitations. I uncovered many more awakenings about myself, yet this was the biggest moment that became a catalyst for sharing intimate details of my life that I hope unravels you further to your greatness.

I realized I gave up on my art dreams to create a career in massage with hidden resentments. I verbalized what I uncovered, received coaching feedback, and took new actions toward my forgotten dreams. I realized that online college was not working for me because I am personable, and I love being around people. I went inward, searched and found what worked better for my life. I discovered Red Rocks Community College in the foothills of the Rocky Mountains of Colorado. When you walk through their doors, you can feel your future unravel before your eyes. The teachers I encountered were keys that unlocked my deepest desires. The LGBTQ center is a thriving and mighty place that embraces everyone, and I felt like I found a home there. The admissions and advising departments made me feel like a celebrity, guided me toward the classes I would need for their Digital Media Journalism degree, and I was officially enrolled back in college after nearly thirty years had passed. I discovered what worked for my life and it empowered me to take this bold new action toward my dreams. I am the artist I always wanted to be, and it is packaged differently than my original vision.

You can apply new techniques, take different actions, or make powerful choices toward your life in what you would like to accomplish. Ask yourself, where would I like to go from here? You can do the same for your life the moment you say, "Go."

I will share key questions I ask every client or friend looking for guidance coaching. Before I do that, let me help set you up for success in this exercise. Find a quiet place, silence or turn off your phone, get comfortable, still and go within.

Close your eyes. Take a deep breath. Connect to the beautiful divine soul that you are.

Take another deep breath. Put your hand on your heart and say this aloud: "I choose to honor myself and all that is me." If you do not feel a shift in yourself, you can choose to repeat that last phrase three times or more if needed.

Take one last deep breath and choose to release any preconceived notions of how you should be. When you are ready, open your eyes. I encourage you to grab a blue pen and journal to answer these questions because it could easily lead to new discoveries. (Here's a fun energy tidbit: a blue pen carries a higher vibration than black.)

- What is not working in your life, or is there something you would like to improve upon?

- If your life is a perfect reflection of you, what does it look like?

- What is working, brings you joy or happiness?

- What old stories are you telling yourself?

- What is your internal dialogue?

- Can you forgive yourself, your past actions and give up judging yourself?

- Are you willing to take a new action today that creates forward momentum for your life?

- Are you willing to give up expectations or what someone else wants your life to look like?

- Can you see anything new for yourself?

- Do you have a support system or people in your life that are uplifting, empowering, and encouraging to you?

- Are you ready?

If you experienced any negative internal dialogue or disbelief in what is possible for yourself, go back and repeat the above exercise until you can make a positive shift. No two people are the same so it could take one time or one hundred times. Remember to be gentle with yourself and record any findings so you can work through what comes up. This is about you, so there is no getting it wrong or right. If I could turn back time, I would have applied all this coaching sooner in my life and saved myself from unnecessary or harmful circumstances. I would tell the young version of me to hold on, be patient, and thrive in life by becoming who I want to be. When we let go of all expectations, old toxic belief patterns, see the facts or truth of self—that is the opening to expansion through awareness.

I am a huge fan of mirror work. While it was some of the hardest self-work I have participated in, it was profoundly empowering. I moved out of covering up every mirror in my house because I thought I was a disgusting monster after my hysterectomy, to beautifully embracing the amazing woman staring back at me. I write empowering messages and affirmations on my mirrors for the continuation of this work to remind me of the winning strides I have made in my life. No one is perfect, and I have days where I struggle, but that is where I take action and call my girlfriends or soul family to remind me when I need it most. I ask for what I need, and you will find this is key for anything in life. Even coaches need coaching at integral times in their lives, and I am no exception to the rule.

Create ten minutes of alone and quiet space. Grab a handheld mirror, blue pen, some paper or a journal and retreat to a well-lit area like the bathroom. Lock the door, so you have zero interruptions. Take a deep breath and connect to yourself.

Take five continuous minutes to stare at yourself in the mirror. Stay silent, observe and notice what comes up. Be mindful of any negative chatter or thoughts and focus on being fully present. Lay the mirror down. Make two columns and record any negative thoughts in the left column.

Take a deep breath. Reconnect. Pick the mirror back up and repeat the process of being fully present with yourself. If a negative thought surfaces again, see how you can positively replace that with uplifting truth. My example of a negative thought: "I am disgusting." Uplifting truth: "My dimples are adorable." After the second five minutes, record your uplifting truths in the right column.

You get bonus points if you can do the five-minute exercise a third time and no negative thoughts surface. You can turn any negative thought into a positive and powerful mantra for yourself.

Everyone needs and should feel heard, seen, valued, safe and appreciated. A basic human need is relating and being with other humans. Over seven billion people on the planet provide a colorful palette of possibilities for the type of souls you surround yourself with. Ask yourself how you would like to be treated. Look at how you are being with others and especially with yourself. Your words carry energy and vibration to your mind, body, spirit, and all those around you. Be mindful of all dialogue.

- Ask yourself, "How am I being in this moment?" Life is full of moments, and it is in a moment that anything can change.

- Assess your progress every day, week, or month by keeping notes or a journal. Set small, realistic goals and create a routine that works best for you. Remember not to make yourself wrong for anything you did and learn from it.

- Your life is yours for the making.

- Stand in your power. Use your voice.

- Leave your impact on the world as the authentic you.

- Pay it forward or carry out little acts of kindness. That alone can help shift your energy in a moment.

No two coaches are the same, so interviewing each other can ensure you have the right team combination for this time in your life. Choose a coach that you resonate with and can challenge you in an empowering way. If something is not working, change it. Be patient with the process that is you in the making. May you always rise no matter what. May the challenges you encounter shape you into a greater purpose and illuminate your path.

CHAPTER

Seven

The Success Cycle
By Elmas Vincent

ELMAS VINCENT

Elmas started his career in corporate America after earning an MBA from Tulane University. After becoming disenchanted with and leaving the corporate world, he shifted his focus and started several businesses in multiple industries. In creating these businesses, Elmas discovered he had a gift and passion in Life Coaching. He has taught a variety of classes at a top, accredited spiritual college including Life Coaching, Hypnotherapy, Neuro-linguistic Programming as well as writing, and teaches multiple business classes to help their students create successful practices.

He currently is a business coach/consultant and speaker at Light-preneurs. Elmas founded Lightpreneurs as a means of helping practitioners who have or are creating a business based on making the world a better, brighter place. You can discover more about Elmas and Lightpreneurs at www.lightpreneurs.com.

The Success Cycle
By Elmas Vincent

What can you learn from a life coach to help you achieve what you want out of life? Everything! This is what good life coaches do for their clients regularly. As a life coach, my job is not to fix anyone or to help them resolve mental/emotional issues. My job is to help my clients achieve what they truly desire and to take them to a higher level in their lives by helping them to discover their answers. Even though my primary focus now is being a business coach and consultant for people in the "light" community, the basic principles of success are the same for anything you might want to achieve.

To help my clients achieve success, I utilize a series of steps to aid them in reaching their goals. When someone is unable to obtain what they want in life, it is because they miss one or more of these steps. By taking yourself through each of these steps, you can accomplish most anything you desire.

My primary job as a life coach is to help people determine what they want because most people don't know what they want. What they do know is what they don't want. They keep focusing on what they don't want, so they keep getting more and more of exactly that. The first step in achieving your desires in life is to *know what you want.* This seems counterintuitive because people think they know what they want. You would think that people know, but after many years of coaching, I have discovered that this is not true.

Until you are clear on what you want and have a vivid image of what it looks like, you are essentially allowing whatever is put on your path to be what you get out of life. The more detailed you can make your goal and include all the senses: seeing it, hearing it, smelling it and tasting it, the more likely you are to experience it as real. Once you start bringing what you want into focus, develop why it is important to you. People like to think of themselves as logical beings, but we are driven by emotion. Emotion is where passion comes from to push us forward.

If you are having difficulty determining what you want in a specific area of your life, you might discover it by looking at its opposite—what you don't want. If you have a vision of what you don't want, ask yourself why you don't want it. What would be the characteristics of *not* that? Focus on the positive aspects of desire rather than avoidance.

Imagine going on a trip and not having a specific destination in mind. The one thing you do know is that you do *not* want to go to San Antonio. You went there once, and it was hot and humid and miserable. You decide to take a trip to anywhere but San Antonio. Chances are you don't leave on a trip because you don't have a destination, but an avoidance of a destination. Instead, what if you look at why you didn't like San Antonio: it was hot and humid. Maybe it would be nice in the fall, winter or spring. Or, you could look at destinations that would be cooler and dryer. Why did you go to San Antonio in the first place? Maybe you can find somewhere that would fulfill that desire with better weather. An alternative might be San Diego because there are lots of things to do there and the weather is nice.

Once you have determined what you truly want, the next step is to *create an action plan*. The old cliché is "when you fail to plan, you plan to fail." Clichés exist because they hold some aspect of truth. Without a plan, how do you know how to start or if you are on the right track once you get going? Having a firm vision of the outcome will help make this process easier. This is where knowing what you want is extremely important. The more detail you have in that goal, the better your plan can be. For bigger goals, make sure to put in place mini-goals that will take you toward the larger goal. These mini-goals will allow you the chance to celebrate those smaller benchmarks to keep you motivated in the journey to what you want. They will also help you see when you are off the target of your objective.

The easiest way to create a successful action plan is by *modeling success*. Find other people who have done what you would like to achieve or something similar and model the steps they took to create their success. By modeling success, you're more likely to develop a winning action plan from the start.

Before you take action, make sure you are coming from *the physiology and psychology of success*. Make sure you are ready for the journey and take the necessary actions for success mentally, physically and emotionally. If you feel defeated before you begin, you are setting yourself up for failure. To be mentally prepared for success is to have a big "why" or reason for accomplishing your goal. We discussed your "why" as part of knowing what you want, and now it is time to utilize the power of that "why" to propel you forward. Make sure your "why" for achieving the goal is strong to help motivate you and keep you in a positive frame of mind. Your "why" is the motivator that will keep you going when obstacles appear.

Make sure you are physically ready for the journey. Some goals might require a great deal of physical stamina or ability:

running a marathon, hiking or other physical accomplishments. For non-physical goals, being physically ready will make you more productive and more likely to achieve success. Getting proper rest, nutrition and self-care to support your body will keep you at the top of your game, not only physically, but also mentally and emotionally.

Many people fail before they start. They are so afraid of failing that they never begin. In Neuro-linguistic Programming, one of the presuppositions is *"there is no failure, just feedback."* How many opportunities do you give a child who is trying to walk for the first time before you say, "This whole walking thing is not for you"? That sounds crazy, yet as adults, we don't give ourselves a chance to try something new due to a fear of failing. If we start looking at a result that is not what we want as feedback on the way to success instead of failure, that simple re-frame can change your life.

Without *action*, nothing happens. With a solid vision of where you want to be and a plan to get there—take action. Once you take the first action step, use your "why" to keep you moving forward to create momentum. Make sure to celebrate the small victories along the way to help keep you motivated and stay in that physiology and psychology of creating success.

One of the critical steps that many people skip is *evaluating progress* along the way. Regular check-ins to see where you are at and if you are on track to achieve your goals will allow you the opportunity to adjust your plan and actions. Evaluate what is working and what is not. Take the feedback to refine your plan to keep you on the right path.

Part of the value of having a life coach is *accountability*. Most people need some form of accountability to keep moving toward their goals. Without a coach, make sure you put tools in place to hold yourself accountable. Use your benchmarks/mini-goals from your plan as opportunities for accountability. Accountability and plan evaluation go hand in hand. Hold yourself accountable for doing the activities in your plan but be willing to adjust those activities if you are doing them and they are not taking you toward your goal. The warning here is to evaluate but also to give the action time to create a result to prevent you from bouncing around from activity to activity without giving them a fair chance to establish the movement necessary.

From this point, it is a matter of cycling through the process until you achieve success. After evaluating where you're at on your journey, adjust your plan if necessary. Keep searching for others who have reached the same or similar goals to find new pieces of the path to model and add to your plan. Make sure you continue to be in the right state physically, mentally and emotionally to help move you toward your end result. Check to make sure your motivations are still strong and reinforce if necessary. Take additional action and then evaluate that action to see if it is taking you where you want to go.

At this point, I would like to offer a couple of caveats. The first is beware of the nay-sayers: "My cousin's best friend's brother tried this once and failed." The nay-sayers think they are protecting us, but you are not your cousin's best friend's brother. By using the success steps outlined here, you are more likely to succeed. Finding someone who has accomplished something close to your goal puts you ahead of the game and increases the likelyhood of your success.

With big goals, there are going to be obstacles. These difficulties are the reason your "why" is so important. By focusing on the positive of what accomplishing the goal will be, it will make it easier to push through the setbacks. By following the steps, you will be able to navigate the challenges and adjust the plan to overcome them.

Finally, having a positive support system can make the journey easier. Forming a mastermind group or sharing the journey with someone who has a similar goal can make the difficult times smoother. It is so easy to become overwhelmed in the process that the solution can seem unattainable. The advantage of having a coach, mentor or other supporter is having their perspective to help you see the forest instead of losing it in the trees.

If you are ready to have the life you want and deserve, take control of your destiny and decide to make it happen. To give yourself the best chance of success, know what you want and create an action plan by modeling the success of others to provide you with a head start. Next, make sure you are operating from a physiology and psychology of success and then take action. Evaluate the results of your actions to see if you are on track. Remember, there is no failure just feedback to use to adjust your plan to keep you moving toward success. Also, use this evaluation process and other procedures to create accountability. Keep cycling through the process until you achieve what you desire.

CHAPTER

Eight

Beyond The Pavement
By Felicia Shaviri

FELICIA SHAVIRI

Felicia Shaviri, a native of Chicago's Englewood District, is on a mission to tell everyone within earshot or afar the importance of the role they play in the world. A former Corrections Deputy turned author and Wellness Coach, Felicia believes every person can turn their life around, regardless of the circumstances. "I stand fast with an unbending belief that there is always an opportunity to learn and grow with every experience. Each experience offers us endless possibilities to live the life we desire." Felicia is a Professional Fitness/Wellness Coach, Certified Life Coach, Reiki

Practitioner, Voice Over Talent and Founder of SheRox Fitness and Wellness.

Connect with Felicia sheroxfitness.com

sheroxfitness.wellness@gmail.com

Acknowledgments

Love and gratitude to my mother, Ola V. Pryor, for planting the seed of curiosity within me as a child. To my dearest Jasmine, I can't thank you enough for all of your loving words of encouragement through each step of this process. You are truly a gift to me and I am so thankful that you chose me.. David (Dr. Buff) Patterson, thank you for believing in me until I could believe in myself. My sister, Debbie Pryor, JV and WC, thank you for keeping me grounded through it all.

Beyond The Pavement
By Felicia Shaviri

After arriving in Seattle in the summer of 1989, it didn't take me long to land a job in customer service working as a reservations agent for Budget Rent-A-Car. After several months of working with the company, we were informed there would be several new employees joining our department. Karen was fresh out of high school, quiet and reserved. Paul, a former gregarious travel agent, could get the entire office to dance to an old school Michael Jackson tune with ease. Then there was Kari.

In her early forties, Kari was twenty years my senior and her voice sounded like nine-inch nails on a chalkboard every time she spoke. Okay, so maybe it wasn't that bad. But for some reason, I was easily irritated by her presence. I had never met anyone that was always so "over the top" and bubbly about everything. She smiled all the time, and for some reason, seemed to think we were friends. I didn't get the memo stating it was okay for her to call me "Falish." Argh.

The reservation center was fairly open with lots of light that flowed into the office, which reminded me of a maze for mice. What I liked best was how laid-back the office was, and the only customer contact that we had was via the telephone. It was located on the second floor of the downtown branch. There were two small offices with doors, and the remainder of the space was made up of makeshift cubicle offices. It was important to be aware of the volume of our voices, so they wouldn't carry over into another call. Everyone in the office got along surprisingly well with little or no drama. I found myself making small talk here and there with Kari and found her quite interesting and genuine.

One day, Kari came into the office, and I could feel that something was different. She brought with her several bags full of stuff, and several minutes later, I could hear her sniffling. I thought maybe she was catching a cold, but I sensed something was wrong and thought maybe she was crying. I put my calls on hold, stood up, looked over the wall of our split cubicle and asked, "Kari are you okay?" She initially said, "Oh nothing, I'm fine." I then said, "Kari, something is wrong. You are clearly crying...what's the matter?"

Kari continued, "Well, my husband just asked me for a divorce after twenty years of marriage." I asked her if that was a good thing or a bad thing. I didn't know what to say. As she blew her nose, I noticed the bags she had brought in were full of things that she was clearing out of their home. I glanced down at her desk and noticed a photograph of a woman running. She was blond with track shorts and a tank that had a number attached. The bottom of the photo read, "L.A. Marathon 1976." I pointed to the photo and asked, "Who is that in the photo?" She replied, "Oh, this one? That's me in my skinny days," as she held up her pinky finger. I was in such awe that I asked her if I could see it, as I extended my hand.

I was fascinated. I didn't know what a marathon was, so I asked her to explain. Kari's mood shifted instantly as I began to ask questions. Up to that point, I had never thought about what a mile was, other than it being eight city blocks. I asked Kari why anyone would want to go out and just run. Then I reminded her that I was from Chicago, and if I was running, there would be a reason for it. I would be running with purpose and not because the sky was blue and it was a nice day. To think that people would run twenty-six miles "just because" was just plain crazy to me, but clearly, they were running regularly in Washington State and I was curious as to why.

Several weeks later, Kari came into the office and she appeared to be adjusting to all the changes that were happening in her life. She was returning to her upbeat, bubbly self once again, which was quite refreshing, and it made me happy. It would also be the day that would cause a dynamic shift in life as I knew it.

Kari brought with her a long-sleeved mock t-shirt and a running bib—for me. She informed me that she had signed us up for the St. Patrick's Day Dash in March. I told Kari I wasn't a runner and she said, "C'mon Falish, it'll be fun and if you start today, you will be a runner by then!" I told her I had never done anything like that before and I didn't know if I could. She again assured me that I could do it and that it wasn't as tough as it seemed, and she believed I could do it even though I didn't. Because I was not convinced, Kari made me an offer. "Okay, Falish. I'll make a deal with you. You do the run, and if you find that you don't like it, you don't have to pay me back the fifteen dollars I paid for registration. But if you do like it, you agree to pay the registration for both of us on the next one." I agreed.

Once I got home, I sat the shirt and bib on the dresser. I would pick it up and look at it then fold it. I repeated this for several days, and then one day after folding it, I decided to put on my sneakers and try jogging. I felt a little awkward and wondered if people would look at me strangely, but I tried it anyway. I jogged from the door of our apartment to the opening entry of the apartment complex which was about two hundred meters, and then I walked back, feeling out of breath. I wondered why people would go out and run just to be running, other than losing weight or getting into shape. Again, I got dressed and repeated the same distance, but this time, I decided to try running back to the apartment door. It wasn't long before I found myself running from the apartment to the fire hydrant, to the stop light, around the apartment complex. I was hooked and could hardly wait for morning to come so that I could get outside for my morning run! Yep, you read that right— I went from jogging to running. I eagerly began to count down the days until the run. I was so excited!

Race Day finally arrived, and my tummy was full of butterflies doing cartwheels. I couldn't believe I was in the middle of all this action. I mean, there were hundreds of people out there dressed in green—and me! One of the most beautiful sounds I would hear was that of the air-gun that signified the start of the race. I was mesmerized by the sounds of laughter, passing conversations, spectators cheering and raising their banners in support of those they knew who were running. I began to feel intoxicated with breathing itself as I effortlessly placed one foot in front of the other over the rolling hills, feeling a series of goose-bump vibrations caused by shouts of joy and the pounding of hundreds of feet echoing off the walls as we made our way through the tunnel. All I kept thinking was, "I am doing it! I'm running!"

As I drove home after the run, I wondered what would be next and that I knew I would give it a try. By shifting my mindset, I not only paid for the next run Kari and I entered, but I found myself venturing into more challenging ones like half marathons, marathon running, and distance relay team runs. Like I said, I was hooked. In time, I would find yet another shift which would lead me to triathlons (swim, bike, run), obstacle course racing, personal training, and ultimately, bodybuilding.

Many years later, I would find myself putting the pieces of my journey together, and I would clearly see the huge impact fitness has had on my mind, body, and spirit. Running became the pathway to clearing my mind through moving meditation. My body thanked me for getting the blood flowing and unloading some of the extra pounds I was carrying, and my spirit came alive as I began to feel the sense of being so alive and free. You never know what any moment may bring. The nudge of a coworker helped me impact the lives of hundreds of others by reminding them to show up as they are and shine their light.

Sometimes we get lost when it comes to deciding which way would be best, but generally, that is a result of looking outside of ourselves for answers that can be found within. Life can be daunting and downright exhausting at times. Whether it's weight loss, relationships, children, career change, or feeling stuck—it doesn't matter. Some individuals can overcome obstacles, break through barriers and reach their set goals alone. Others may require someone else's assistance to get them started which often has a great deal to do with the thoughts and views of themselves and how they see the world around them. We may not see our goals as attainable, so we either give up, don't follow through completely or we stop setting them. Put one foot in front of the other and see where it will lead. You never know until you try! As a MindShift Coach, I help to guide clients in the direction of reconnecting to themselves and the world by discovering the importance of their existence in it. We are all surrounded by mirrors which help us to see if we are living fully by how we show up. Living our best life begins from within and although the work required may be challenging, it is often the most rewarding. Have you ever wanted to try or experience something only to find that you've talked yourself out of it with the next thought? One of the first and most important steps to change is stepping outside of our comfort zones. Growth is something that happens as we learn to become comfortable with being uncomfortable.

Getting caught in the webs of fear stops so many from attempting to put forth any effort. Instead of throwing your ideas, dreams or thoughts out with the trash, try thinking back to something that you dreamt of doing or found yourself being a little bit curious about. Now ask yourself what is the worst that could happen if you Googled some information on the subject. Seek out someone that you can speak with on the subject, check out a book from the library or watch a YouTube video or take a class. Try setting aside a few minutes in the morning or before bed to visualize what it would feel like to have achieved the goal.

Over the course of my personal journey as well as in coaching clients, I have found the quote by Buddha "We are shaped by our thoughts; we become what we think" to be one of the truest statements I have ever experienced in my life, and my heart is full and excited for you as I believe in you too. It doesn't matter where you are on your path, just remember you can shift your thinking and create the world in which you would like to live. There is no one else that knows you as well as you do. So, get up, get out and get it done! This is your life and you got it covered even if it doesn't always feel that way!

CHAPTER

Nine

Shining The Light:
Releasing Resentments
For Freedom And Joy!
By Gretchen Stecher

GRETCHEN STECHER

The mother of two outstanding young men, Gretchen earned her master's degree after they were successfully launched. Having traversed mountains and valleys, ferocious storms, barren deserts and winding rivers, she claims her doctorate is in feeling the fear and doing it anyway. Gretchen was certified as a sexual assault and domestic violence counselor in 2001, served as adjunct faculty in the Graduate School of Psychology at Naropa University, is a certified somatic trauma specialist, and EMDRII trained. She currently has a private practice as a psychotherapist and life coach in Boulder, Colorado.

Over 20 years as a 12-step recovery veteran, Gretchen's expertise is helping clients experience freedom and joy by releasing resentments and practicing love-based states. She delights in co-creating sacred ceremonies to access spiritual connection. A catalyst for the revitalization of humans, Gretchen is humbled and honored to hold the light for evoking and recovering the essence of each person.

www.soulshinecolorado.com
gretchen@soulshinecolorado.com
720-500-5474

Acknowledgments

A forever, full-bodied thank you to Gloria Alexander for being my consistent light. Huge gratitude to Bev and Bill for their support now, and Betsy—much love. Also, to Peter and Danny, for their love and connection. For the unswerving friendship, tears, laughter, and wild wonderment with Jeannie Church. To my clients, who've taught me mountain-loads. Deep appreciation to Betty Wall and other teachers, including Katie Asmus and Sweigh Spilkin for their complete commitment to what wants to happen, to source, to ceremony and nature, and manifesting medicine. To Laura Walker, divine editor. To brilliant Shara Howie. Heartfelt thank you Jan Shapan for your generosity and support. To Joey Klein. And a heartful bow to my fierce, tender, magnificent soul who never gives up.

Shining The Light:
Releasing Resentments
For Freedom And Joy!
By Gretchen Stecher

For a long time, I blamed my self-loathing, "negaholism" (focus on the negative), and horrible self-talk on my parents. After all, I grew up in an alcoholic home, experiencing a high level of resentments (oh the thick tension in the air), social isolation and authoritarianism ("yes sir," "no ma'am," obedience comes first.) However, after years of criticizing (20's to about 50 years old), I saw that blaming my parents wasn't helping me at all. Not only that, my complaining, wishful thinking (if only they'd change), and resenting wasn't changing *them*. I can undeniably report that those things work well for staying stuck! With my face flat against the wall, I finally accepted that I needed to do something different if I truly wanted a better life. It was a serious challenge for me. I discovered that deep down I felt terrified to do something different. All I had known was the misery of suffering as a victim.

My deepest longing for wellness (the marvelous life force in us all) eventually brought me the support I needed to claw my way up past the bottom of the black abyss of misery. I'd begun my journey into the light. I lived through a destructive cult, divorce, letting go of my two boys, homelessness, bankruptcy, debilitating physical injury, and addictions. I needed all of those to grow the strength and perspective to accept my own divine magnificence, to glow in the glory of it, and to help others evoke and radiate theirs!

One of the bigger lessons I learned during my ascent journey was the poisonous venom produced by resentments. This venom becomes lodged in the system of the "resenter," *not*—as the thoughts attached to resentments would have us believe—in the "resentee" (the person who is resented). I'll explain why, offer a way to discover your resentments, and give a technique to begin releasing this poison.

Resentments: What and Why

Resentments are a cluster of fear-based emotions (anger, many shades of fear, often shame and guilt) plus the thoughts that go with them. The primary emotion that shows up with resentments is anger. It is not anger about what's happening in the present, however. Resentments are a backward-looking emotional experience because they're based on past situations. These emotions and thoughts can be activated or triggered by a current circumstance.

A primary function of our brains is "linking." When something gets our attention, the brain immediately searches for something similar from the past. This capacity to link or connect similarities occurs for several reasons: to make sense of what's happening in the present (to understand it) or for protection. The most important thing is to protect from danger, survival being the first order of business for every living organism. Linking also helps with efficiency. Rather than having to figure out from the beginning what something means or if it's a threat, if it feels familiar and safe, the body doesn't have to go into fight or flight mode. Or, if it is like a familiar threat from the past, then the alarm is sounded, and the defenses come online. This all happens unconsciously and at crazy-fast speed.

Let's look at how it works defensively. An interaction with someone triggers the memory of a similar situation from the past, and the mind concludes that what's happening is enough like past circumstances that the same protective reaction is needed now. When the defenses are mounted in the body, our capacity to appraise and to think creatively go offline. We react—*boom*! What if the unconscious mechanisms have mistakenly evaluated the experience and there's no real danger? It can be confusing because the body is reacting like there *is* real danger. It doesn't mean we're stupid or don't want to change. It means all systems are functioning naturally from the oldest part of the brain's point of view. Bringing the newer brain back online—the prefrontal cortex, wherein lies the decision-making capacity, the ability to pause and step back long enough to see if there's actual danger—is what we're needing in the moment. Blaming and contemplating how we've been wronged (typical resentment thoughts) don't work for that.

Here's what I learned from extensive research on resentments:

- They infiltrate all relationships, cross culturally.
- When resentments are present in *any* relationship, each one affects *all* relationships, including connection to oneself and the divine.
- They include assumptions that keep us separate from others in our minds.
- They block natural energy flow in our bodies, contributing to diseases.
- It has been said that resentments are at the root of terrorism.

I found that there are no redeeming qualities about this cluster of emotions and thoughts. I found no one offering relief from these nasty critters. I knew the detrimental effect they had on my life and the lives of others, so I've made it my mission to help people feel the freedom and joy of releasing resentments.

There's nothing wrong with any emotion, especially anger. When we allow it to run through the body like a wave, growing big then gradually dwindling, it can complete. When there's a resentment, fear-based emotions race around on a hamster wheel, thoughts fueling them so that they don't complete. Thus, the body thinks that danger is constant, doing its job of discharging the biochemicals needed for fight or flight. This eventually erodes parts of our internal systems which contributes to diseases. Sound like a good reason to release resentments?

How Do I Know If I Have Resentments?

Let's start with how to determine if resentments are present. Below is The Resentment Assessment, a tool I use to begin the process of releasing hamsters from the wheel. The questions help reveal current resentments as well as shadow-lurkers. They can be sneaky critters, justifiably rationalized and culturally supported. Perhaps it is time for you to consider whether your joy, serenity and freedom, the quality of your relationships, and your ability to be your true self are compromised by resentments.

The Resentment Assessment

A way to uncover resentments hidden inside is to ask the questions listed below. When we talk about a person or situation, even from years ago, and there's a rise in the body's energy (i.e., heat, tingling, clenching, louder voice) or we notice that we're holding on to our righteous position, we've probably landed one. Approach the naming with curiosity and a quest for clarity without judgment. Judging creates tension and blocks honest expression. It's good to know what's there.

1. Do I blame (myself, others, or what happened) for my lack of something or for my misery?
2. Do I feel entitled to something that someone else says is not mine?
3. Am I *still* mad at someone after they did something that I specifically asked them not to do?
4. Do I feel like I've been treated unfairly by someone with power over me? Do I long for revenge or an apology but feel powerless about getting it?
5. Do I think that a person is doing something to deliberately upset me?
6. Do I keep asking or expecting someone to do something that they've never done?
7. Can I not let go of being mad at someone for stomping all over my self-worth?
8. Am I fuming because a person who knew I'd say yes (even though they knew I didn't want to do it) asked anyway?
9. Am I holding a grudge, or angry about a situation from long ago?

For many people, at least one of these questions has either a familiar ring or a resounding *yes*. It is great news to be able to name these hamsters because resentments are kept alive in a cycle. An interaction flares up anger (usually mixed with other fear-based emotions like shame, anxiety, a sense of unfairness or guilt), which then fuels specific thoughts (i.e., memories of a similar incident or other wrongs done by the same person) that re-ignite the emotions, and the hamster wheel keeps spinning. Take a moment to jot down some of the thoughts that come up when you're feeling resentments.

Resentments serve as a protective shield, keeping us from feeling the fear-based emotions underneath them, which we consider painful or scary. When we begin naming and feeling those emotions in a safe environment, we can release our grip on the shield, breathe more easily, and feel better. It is strongly recommended to seek the support of a person who, having experienced a process for letting go of resentments themselves, can guide you in your discovery and releasing process.

You can access The Resentment Assessment on my website as a handout, if you'd like. When you ask yourself the questions and you're able to name a resentment (i.e., "I resent my mother for blaming me for her unfulfilled life") then we've got something to work with. Yes!

Now that you can recognize when a resentment is poisoning the present moment, erroneously signaling danger and hijacking centered thinking, let's do the next step. Here's a way to start letting go of resentments, and have serenity in personal connections, including the most important relationship—with yourself. It's a technique you can use by yourself to begin the releasing process. I call it Tap and Clap:

Tap and Clap

1. Hold the person in your mind.
2. Hold the resentment in your thoughts and body. (Notice the thoughts that go along with it. Feel the emotions and physical sensations that it produces.) Let yourself get in touch with all aspects of the resentment, as much as you can.
3. While holding it inside (or picturing it near you; see examples below), do the following physical movements:
    a. Tap your left foot on the floor (lift it up, put it down).
    b. Tap your right foot on the floor.

c. Tap your left thigh once with your right hand (touch, let go).
d. Tap your right thigh once with your left hand.
e. Clap your hands together twice.
f. Tap your left upper arm once with your right hand (touch, let go).
g. Tap your right upper arm once with your left hand.
h. Repeat a) through g) in the same order.
i. Have as much *fun* with this as you can. Play with it—try it with music!

There's no need to rush it. Go slowly at first to get the feel and rhythm. If holding everything inside feels like too much, try these alternatives:

- Put the resentment (with feelings, thoughts, even images) near you in a bubble or a box or on a bench.
- Imagine that you have a third hand or even a tail that is holding the resentment while you move. Be creative and see what works for you. *What works is what counts.*

This can also be done with a partner: follow the steps above but instead of tapping crisscross on your upper arms, tap the crisscross with your partner's palms—right palms together, then left palms together. Do the technique as many times as you like, but no need to overexert. Again, play with it! The more light-heartedness and joy you bring to it, the better.

Check in before starting Tap and Clap and rate your level of activation when you think about the person and situation. How irritated are you feeling? Rank it on a scale of 1 to 10, where 10 is extremely activated. There are no detrimental side effects from this technique. Use it as often as you want. If you notice that the resentment pops up again, rate the level of activation, then do Tap and Clap. Rate your level of activation again when you've finished. Trust yourself. You'll know when you're done for now.

Why does Tap and Clap work? The simple answer is that we're rewiring the brain by pairing a new, playful memory and love-based emotions with a person or situation that was linked with fear-based emotions and thoughts (i.e., resentments). Love-based and fear-based energy cannot occupy the same space, like oil and water. The more you overlay fear-based memories with love-based experiences, the stronger the rewiring in the brain becomes. Everyone I know who has used this technique has had a significant reduction in the activation level of their resentment. Let me know how well it works for you!

To go even deeper into releasing resentments, especially for those long-term ones that have been stuck in the shadowy crags for ages, there's my powerfully transformational group, *Shine the Light: Release Resentments for Freedom and Joy! Shine the Light* gives participants an opportunity to learn to be totally honest with themselves without judgment, reaching into new places with curiosity in a safe environment. As each person becomes immersed in the special writing recipe for unpacking resentments, they grow their capacity to observe their thoughts, emotions, behaviors and reactions. This develops the ability to pause and consider conscious responding versus reacting from imprinted, automatic patterns. It uncovers thinking and behavior patterns that underpin distressful self-talk and relationship difficulties, particularly ones beneath addictions and trauma. Empowerment reigns when we replace old patterns with realistic, love-based choices. Curiosity and radical acceptance are fostered. An individualized self-compassion recipe is created for each participant to use forever. The group sharing helps participants experience that they're not alone. Body awareness techniques for remembering and self-care are practiced. Somatic (body-based) techniques add a layer of effectiveness that accelerates transformation. Handouts are included. *Shine the Light* group is a life-changer and has already helped many women completely shift relationships. One woman with a long-held resentment towards her sister had tried for 15 years to let it go, using various methods. She was delighted to be freed from this obsession, able to move on with her life after going through the group process! Another had deep-seated resentments (about 50 years' worth) toward her mother, causing her much distress, as mom was on her death bed. After doing *Shine the Light*, she was able to release the resentments and accept her mother, who waited for her to arrive before transitioning. The daughter lovingly let mom go, allowing for a peaceful crossing over the veil.

Shine the Light is a gender-specific group (participants in each group identify as the same gender) that meets weekly, generally for four months. I invite you to connect with me if you are interested in hearing more about the group. I'd love to hear about your experience with Tap and Clap.

You are a magnificent being who has courageously chosen to spend time learning on earth in human form for a while. When we let go of what we've known, we can move into the joy of who we really are! May you recognize your blessings.

CHAPTER

Ten

Fill It Up With Joy
By Heather V. Dunning

HEATHER V. DUNNING

Heather V. Dunning offers healing collaborations built on authenticity and intuitive empathy. Like those she serves, Heather aspires to grow and evolve past pains, patterns and limiting beliefs. As a wife, mother, daughter, sister, friend, and all around people-lover, she finds gifts of gratitude in blessings and challenges. Admired by clients for her contagious and untouchable passion for her work, renowned for her ability to introduce individuals to new ways of thinking, believing, and living, and beloved for guiding people through compassionate, understanding and soul-shifting experiences. Heather is trained and certified in a number of healing modalities. She's worked as a joy guide and body whisperer for 20 years. Based in Richmond, Va., Heather serves clients around the world, helping them discover purpose and connect with inner truth through an unstructured and holistic approach. Learn more about her offerings, client reviews, and contact her through her website: www.HeatherVDunning.com

Acknowledgments

I dedicate this joy-filled chapter to one of the most loving, compassionate, joyful souls I've had ever had the pleasure of meeting, birthing, and dancing through this life with. Grace, remember: Joy is your essence and by being fabulous you, you inspire and invite others to do the same.

Fill It Up With Joy
By Heather V. Dunning

What is joy? Do we really know?

I ask that as Marie Kondo and her Netflix series, *Tidying Up with Marie Kondo*, grows within our cultural conversation. If you are unfamiliar with Kondo, or her patented KonMari method for organizing your home, she challenges you to individually hold something you own while asking yourself, "Does this spark joy?" You ultimately keep the things that do and discard the things that don't.

We watch everyday folks ask themselves should it stay or should it go now? If it stays, will there be double? If it leaves will they be troubled? People cling to items that include old, unworn concert t-shirts, uninspiring artwork, sentimental, handmade items gifted from granny, and dusty sports trophies from decades ago. I wonder if they fully understand what they are being asked to spark?

Joy can be a confusing concept and let's face it: if we can't understand joy, we can't cultivate it, elevate it, or even celebrate it.

So, what exactly is joy?

Joy is an essence, an overwhelming vibration, and it's undeniable. To me, joy is the ability to exhale effortlessly, engage an inner grin and be completely present in that moment. When experiencing joy, you are in alignment with the lightness of your soul. Joyfulness is a lighthouse guiding you out of dark, foggy waters back to your true self. It can feel blissful, elated or exuberant, or peaceful.

As I lay peacefully on my sun-kissed deck, with my beloved sleeping 12-year-old snuggled up beside me while writing this chapter, I am filled with the gift of joy.

I was taught long ago, and have since confirmed many times, that joy is our highest vibration— higher than both gratitude and even love. We tend to think of love as the end all, be all. The Beatles sang to us that love was all we need. However, joy is our highest vibe. We can give and receive love and not necessarily be embodying a state of joyfulness.

Joy can be confused with happiness which, though similar, is not the same thing.

Happiness is mood-based, a superficial, fleeting wave in the ocean and often dependent on circumstance. Joy is deeper, felt on a soul level, and encompasses the complexities and depth of the entire ocean, not the ever-changing tides. People often struggle, however, at making that distinction. In fact, when clients come to see me, they use the word "happy" a lot. And I explain that happiness is waning; it comes and it goes, but you want something sustaining. You want to step into your essence of joy.

Happiness can come from feeling like we are appreciated and accepted by others. Joy can arise as a byproduct of your deep love and acceptance for yourself. For those that suffer from chronic pain, joy can often be found in pain-free moments of connection with loved ones or ease in everyday tasks. Dancing with a beloved, lifting your toddler, dressing without restriction, and even a restful sleep, to name a few.

That kind of joy—the kind that comes from being around people who energize, the joy that numbs physical pain or discomfort, the kind that creates mindfulness of the *now*—is far too infrequent in our lives.

Three Aspects of Joy

Our relationship with joy typically falls into one of three categories:

- The first is the person who forgets their joy from time to time, and can benefit from being reminded how to tune into it and cultivate it;
- The second is the person who is so severely blocked from joy that they have forgotten it can even exist for them;
- The third is the person who lives in an abundance of joy, perhaps to the point that his or her authenticity is questioned because people in the other two categories can't conceive of such overflowing joy.

Below, I want to describe someone in each category and offer an exercise he or she can practice to expand and celebrate their joy. None of these aspects are good or bad; they're different perspectives. It is common for each of us to experience all of them at some point throughout our lives.

Aspect 1: Remembering Joy

The power of the mind is underutilized. It's important to remember this as we all risk being swept up in the currents of life.

We can harness that power by calling up one joyous memory to perform what's called an anchoring technique. This process creates a point that you can squeeze on your body to access the essence of joy. A typically attainable spot is between the thumb and pointer finger of either hand. This is also a headache relief point, so you can anchor positivity and release pressure in the body at the same time.

Begin by recalling a memory of when you knew you experienced joy, when it emanated throughout you. It could be a sunset at the ocean, sunrise over the mountains, time with a loved one or snuggled with a beloved pet. You may also choose the simplicity of a delicious meal, a hot shower, planting in your garden, or even a quiet walk in the morning light.

Let me offer an example: my connection to the ocean. Every time I'm at the ocean, I experience the essence of joy—even if the elements of the day leave me unhappy. Maybe the ocean is too rough, wind too fierce, sun too hot, or those pesky biting flies are treating you like a Thanksgiving feast. None of those details, or my unhappiness with them, can ever diminish the joy I feel at the ocean. If I'm anchoring joy, I imagine sitting in front of the ocean and breathing in that salty air.

First, ground yourself. Sit up nice and tall, feet flat, spine aligned. Take a nice deep inhale and connect with your body and breath, while recalling your joy-filled memory.

Next, visualize that moment when you experienced joy—not happiness, but the state of presence where nothing is being done or given. You don't have to do anything to feel joy. It's your soul's vibration, your essence, and an overwhelming feeling that washes over you like a waterfall.

Connect with the area of your body where joy arises from within. Breathe it in. Begin to pick up the pace and rhythm by pumping up your breath like a bicycle tire. Once you feel you have maximized the essence, squeeze the designated point in your hand. On the exhale, send that vibration of joy throughout your entire body to each and every cell, muscle, joint, and organ.

You might be asking yourself, what is the point of this? Every single emotion that you have ever felt in your life is anchored into your body somewhere. When I first breathed in joy, it was in my chest and shoulders. When I take that vibration and anchor it into a squeezable, reachable spot for myself, even if I'm not feeling that vibration throughout my day, I can squeeze that spot and trigger that vibration.

You can use this anchoring technique to access any positive emotion. If you want to feel confidence, love, joy, peace, or clarity, think of a time when you experienced it. Sense where you feel it in your body, use your breath, and increase the vibration. When you reach the highest vibration, you're going to squeeze the spot where you wish to anchor.

Aspect 2: Blocked from Joy

Some people say they cannot experience joy. It feels like fiction, or unattainable, to them. They will swear they lack a single memory to look to for that anchoring exercise.

For most of these people, the essence of joy is not an unknown but rather inaccessible; they're blocked.

Those blocks can be the result of traumas, abuse, neglect, PTSD, or the unexpected death of a loved one. These painful occurrences may have changed the course of their life, steering them farther away from the light of joy.

Let's say that somebody, until age 12, experiences nothing but joy. She has a beautiful family, a great home in a good community, and a great life. She is an athlete who earns great grades— everything ideal you could possibly imagine. Sadly, soon after she turns 12 years old, one of her parents tragically dies unexpectedly.

That loss turns her life completely upside down. And in that moment, her joy goes incognito, or dormant, and does so deeply.

This formerly joyous girl begins building up all this animosity, resentment and even rage, depression, and isolation. And then she reads this book and says that she can't remember a time she experienced joy because the moment that tragedy occurred, it blocked her from those previous years of joy.

I have worked with clients who honestly believe that every day of their lives have been nothing but misery.

If that is you, this exercise might be challenging, but not impossible. I recommend modifying it by selecting someone in your life who you know emanates joy, or experiences many joyous moments, or that you maybe feel a little bit lighter in their presence. Almost everyone has at least one person like that in their lives, hopefully.

Sit up nice and tall, feet flat, spine aligned, head upright while breathing fully into your body. Same as before.

Now, visualize that person who you see as joyous, even if for a moment in time when you saw them experiencing pure joy. Once you see that person embodying their joy to the fullest and glowing from it, you then visualize yourself stepping into that person's body and feeling the vibration through them.

Aspect 3: An Abundance of Joy

For some people, an abundance of joy can be a challenge. Those who experience and share their joy freely and easily are sometimes met with skepticism from others who are less in touch with their joy.

That was my experience when I was younger. In my late teens and early 20s, I always felt like I brought the positivity. Yet, my friends would accuse me of being a Disney tour guide, or Julie, the Love Boat cruise director. They would accuse me of somehow faking my joy, as if that served a purpose. This happened not only once, but many times. People couldn't believe that somebody could be that joyful.

As you know, the world can feel heavy, dense, and agitating. When we struggle through that to survive, we don't know what to make of someone who's thriving, and it can be tempting to doubt their sincerity. For those being doubted, it is tempting to surrender their joy to fit into the low-vibe tribe. No one can take joy from you. However, we can convince ourselves that they did.

Let's say you're out and about, reveling in your joy business and a Negative Nancy tries to diminish your energy by criticizing your elation and calling it inauthentic. In that harsh moment of judgment, you have a choice to make: you can either allow that energy to steal your joy or you can reclaim your joy as a gift and metaphorically share that gift with that person without ever having to say or do anything. Imagine leaving your gift of joy with them so it's there for them when and if they're ready to receive it.

Or, maybe we use the analogy of cookies, because who doesn't love cookies?

Let's pretend that you bake delicious cookies in an air of love and light, and these cookies are golden. What happens if you offer one of the cookies to someone and they don't accept it?

You don't have to allow that person's lack of appetite for your joy cookies to minimize the amount of joy, love and gratitude that you put into them. You still have these amazing cookies. Someone else will enjoy them, or you can keep their yumminess for yourself.

After all, that's the purpose of the first exercise. By anchoring joy from a memory, or when you experience it in real time, you create your joy cookies for when you feel depleted. When someone is causing you to doubt your authenticity around joyfulness, you have it there.

Why Joy Matters

Why does this matter? Why do you need to cultivate, elevate, and celebrate your joy? It's about feeling that essence, sure, but it's more than that.

Joy connects us with our soul's purpose in life. If we're not at joy, we're underneath it. And if we're underneath it, there's a disconnection, be it a disconnection from our body, our energy field, our journey, our peace, or even our self-love.

Joy is a beacon, aligning you with your soul's lighthouse.

When you find yourself asking the big questions of life, like, "What's my purpose? Why am I here? What am I supposed to be doing?" the essence of joy is the indicator of whether you're on the right path.

Don't discount the value of that, even if the essence of joy feels, at times, elusive. Many of the clients I see have become unwittingly complacent in the dark and heavy feelings of depression, fatigue, exhaustion, isolation, sadness, grief, and even considerations of suicide.

The world feels so heavy today, as it has for the past decade or so, that many people aren't experiencing their joy. They're not even close to it. They're not thriving, they're merely surviving. And the idea of joy being so elusive, they're existing on auto-pilot.

They can't even imagine a life where they would go from a survival mentality to a thriving one. They've become so attuned to a world of colorless khaki and lifeless gray that they've forgotten about the infinite rainbow of life's deep, rich colors. Those heavy vibrations weigh us down like a negative anchor.

Holding on to our essence of joy can be challenging, given what we're facing. Yet, it's entirely worthwhile. We want to keep using the lightness of joy, gratitude and love. They're very light, so they don't always have the weight to pull up the heaviness. If we turn on our joy-light, the darkness dissipates.

Make a Joy Date

Ask yourself what spaces in your life and your body could use a little of joy's sunshine and lightness. Start to create action steps on all the creative ways you can explore your relationship with joy and her ever-inspiring glow. Remember: whether for a minute, a day, a season or a lifetime, it's the *quality* of joy, not the quantity; the *being,* not the doing. Be joyful!

CHAPTER

Awakening Awareness By Calming The Mind
By JamieLynn

JAMIELYNN

As an Empowerment Coach, JamieLynn empowers lives, one voice at a time. After ten years of personal development and leadership training, she founded Arise Empowered, LLC which offers coaching programs and individualized coaching.

JamieLynn was trained in public speaking and delivered a talk on thriving after sexual abuse on the DEBx stage in front of hundreds, and is featured in the DEBx newsletter. She hosts the Empower-ment Seminar and the Breakthrough & Thrive Summit. JamieLynn's passion for empowering those who have endured sexual abuse stems from her experiences of being sexually abused

by five of her cousins. Through her healing and discovering her voice, JamieLynn saw that she was making a difference for others and has chosen to assist others in finding their path to healing.
AriseEmpowered.org
JamieLynn.AriseEmpowered@gmail.com
715-600-1926

Acknowledgments

The support of others ensures success. I am grateful for: my husband Mike, who has been at my side throughout the entirety of my healing journey; my girls, who remind me of the excitement of the world; my family, who gifted me understanding and taught me unconditional love; my coaches over the years who saw the possibilities in me and the three therapists who gifted me a listening ear and guiding light: Carol, Jim, and Mildred; friends whose love and support allowed me to feel bold and brave: Mellissa Z., Mellissa M., Christal H., Jon T., Gordon G., Davy L., Rob C., and to those who have passed: Becky W. and Katie B. Thanks to your souls for seeing me and accepting me. A special thanks to Rob. Also, thanks to my editor, Vicky.

Awakening Awareness
By Calming The Mind
By JamieLynn

As an empowerment coach, my job is to ensure that my clients are aligned with their lives and work with them to make their lives extraordinary. I start by awakening their awareness to themselves and their communities.

Awareness is the ability to see past what you already know or think you know. It means being present in your life, with others, and on your tasks. It's more than being focused; it's a way of living with focus to create action.

Awareness allows your mind to open and expand into your life, seeing the people you love and cherish for all they are. You are likely thinking, "How is this accomplished?" First, I recommend you start small. Here is an exercise you can do right now.

Take a moment and listen to your surroundings. It's likely you have your eyes open. Now take a moment and close your eyes and listen. Do you notice anything new?

Let's bring the focus to your body. Close your eyes, take a deep breath and relax. Tell your shoulders to relax, and keep working your way down through your body all the way to your toes. With each body part, take a deep breath. This should only take a couple of minutes.

When you have finished, take one last deep breath and open your eyes. Being aware of your surroundings and your body is an amazing place to begin awakening your awareness.

Being with Yourself Exercise

1. Close your eyes and take a deep breath.

2. Whisper to your body, "Relax."

3. Focus on the areas of your body that are uncomfortable or in pain and with a deep breath, one at a time, tell each of those areas to relax.

4. Next, bring your focus to the top of your head, and work your way down to your toes, whispering to each area to relax.

5. Take one more deep breath and open your eyes.

How does your body feel? Do you feel calm? If you enjoyed this practice, it's a good one to use throughout your day. If you choose a specific part of your body and tell it to relax with deep breathing, it will only take a few seconds. During those few seconds, the current stresses will release.

Let's take a moment to look at how our awareness affects others. When in conversation, do you notice your thoughts wandering? At times, you are paying attention when an idea pops into your mind, and you find your thoughts somewhere else as the person you are talking to continues with their story. Here is a practice I use to bring myself to be present in the moment. This practice will improve with use.

Awareness with Others Exercise

Bring your focus to your thoughts. Tell yourself to stop thinking. How long did that last? Thoughts are always there. However, we can quiet our thoughts by shifting what we are focusing on. This takes practice, and the trick to being present with another is to repeat what they say in your mind as they are talking.

At first, this practice seems as though it takes a lot of effort, but with practice, it becomes second nature.

We can practice this by reading. Instead of reading words quickly and skimming across the page with your eyes, try looking at each word fully. This is an example of how you can train yourself to listen to another. As the conversation continues, you will notice your eye contact with them is strong. You will find that you can see yourself in the stories they are sharing, and in the end, you might have something to add or advise. Awareness is not something that comes naturally; it is a practice, and in time, you can be a master of awareness.

Authenticity Awareness

Authenticity requires us to remove our masks. Look into your life for a moment. Do you ever notice that how you behave with family and close friends is dramatically different from how you behave with co-workers or other social groups? Your natural and first response is likely, "No way." Or, "Of course, I can't act like that at work." These are valid responses.

To be authentic is to know who you are, say what you intend, and be as you are without the influence of doubt, fear, or concern for being judged. Authenticity is living your truth in all areas of your life.

Authenticity is based on facts. It's accurate and reliable. Inauthenticity is lacking full reality or sincerity. Most of us are unknowingly inauthentic. We wear a mask in certain crowds.

How do you distinguish your inauthentic self from your authentic self? You have to be willing to look, discover and transform. As a child, my inauthentic way of being was to be shy, quiet, and keep my thoughts to myself. My authentic child wanted to tell you stories until your ear fell off from overuse. In my adult life, there are times when I choose to keep my thoughts to myself and times when I choose to be outspoken. Both are authentic ways of being because I don't have thoughts of my own or comments from others stopping or suppressing who I am. I allow myself to be who I am, free from worry, judgment, and concern. Occasionally, old thought patterns will show up, and in that case, I look at who I am committed to being now.

Take out a sheet of paper and answer these questions: who are you committed to being? Who do you want to be? Ask yourself, "When did I start being shy, angry or sad?" Those emotions may not belong to you. They may have been placed upon you by someone else or by a situation that resulted in you formulating an understanding that life operated a certain way. When we observe when this mindset began, we have an opportunity to create something new.

For me, it was first grade. The sun was beaming into the class room, and I felt amazing. The teacher asked a question, and I had the definite answer. My hand shot up, the first and only student to do so. I said clearly, loudly and confidently the answer to the question. Her response was, "That was great! I could clearly hear you. Okay class, all of you need to raise your voices when you speak, just like Jamie." I felt their glares at me. I felt that the rest of the class hated me for being perfect at that moment. My mom would often tell me that being better than others was bad and wrong. From that day on, I wanted to be quiet, shy, and not want to ever raise my hand again, in fear of others' judgments and wanting to be liked.

Over time, I had forgotten about that moment and my inauthentic self was created. From then on, I would suppress my true self until I took the time to look at where I was being inauthentic. This is not a natural conversation to have, however, it is an amazing question to answer that will grant you the key to being free to express and be who you are.

Take a moment to look in your life. Do you have a similar story to discover?

When I discovered this story, I had an insight. I had a choice. I could choose to be shy and inauthentic (which served its purpose for a time) or I could choose to state my mind, speak up, and be my authentic self. No matter the choice, it is valid. I am not wrong for being shy, but I am also not wrong for speaking my mind. To take it one step further, others are not wrong in how they respond when I speak out or choose to be shy.

Who are you going to be—authentic or inauthentic? Remember each one is valid. You have a choice.

Forgiveness Awareness

The greatest gift you can grant yourself is forgiveness. Forgive others, and forgive yourself. Forgiveness is not about those who have caused you harm; it's about you no longer carrying the burden of the harm caused. Forgiveness does not come easily. First, we start by breaking down the process of what forgiveness can be.

The definition of forgiveness is to stop the feeling of being angry or resentful toward someone for an offense, flaw or mistake. Here is the funny thing about holding on to the anger and resentfulness—by doing so we give the person who has offended us power over us.

The anger is of them; thus, the power is in their hands. If you give yourself the gift of forgiveness, you grant yourself freedom from the burden to carry the pains. Let's take a look at the steps to forgiveness.

In writing or through a conversation, create a list or write a story of what happened, what was said, and what you think happened. There is a difference between what happened and what you think happened. I encourage you to take a look at both authentically. What happened are the facts. What you think happened is the emotional reaction to the facts. Both are valid and important for this work.

Once you have listed it all out, and without reading it over, ask yourself if you are ready to heal.

If you are ready, move on to the next step. Acknowledge the impacts on yourself, and any impacts you think there were for the one who offended you. Examples of impacts might be the resulting feelings of upset or a physical impact that may have occurred.

Is there anything you would be interested in telling the person who caused you harm? Is there anything you wish to hear from that person? Is there anything that you can take responsibility for (not as a form of blame, but as a form of power)? Write the answer to each question.

The last step is to ask yourself this final question: are you ready to forgive?

Forgiveness may need to be done one moment at a time. It could also be a one-time statement. I offer you the task to create a declaration for yourself. A declaration is a place to stand. In some cases, the declaration can become a needed boundary and a place to hold for yourself. "I declare I forgive (name here)." Say nothing else after. If there is more to say, work your way through the process until you can say with a strong mind, "I declare I forgive (name here)."

It is your choice if you will tell the person who has caused you harm that you forgive them. It isn't necessary to tell them. Forgiveness is a tool used for healing. Forgiveness is for *your* benefit.

Forgiveness Exercise

1. Write out what happened. (Fact)

2. Write out what you think happened. (Emotional Fact)

3. Are you ready to heal?

4. What are the impacts of the circumstance on yourself?

5. What are the possible impacts of the one who offended you?

6. Is there anything you wish to tell the person who offended you?

7. Is there anything you would like the person to tell you?

8. Where can you take responsibility as a sense of power?

9. Forgive, as a gift to yourself.

Fear is that feeling in the pit of the stomach, that thing that seems to hit us in the face. We freeze or get angry when fear is present. While fear could stop you, these next conversations will assist you in analyzing the fears you experience and perhaps erase some of your fears.

Suppression of stress creates unpleasant habits and irrational fears. In this section, we will look at two writing exercises that with use and practice will release the suppression over time. Separating yourself from what frustrates you or causes you stress is a brilliant way to release suppressed stresses that can date back to early childhood.

Frustration Writing

1. Set a timer for five minutes.

2. Each morning, write out any frustrations you are facing.

3. Don't worry about spelling, grammar or penmanship.

4. Rip up what you have written and put it in the garbage.

Gratitude Writing

Once you have completed your Frustration Writing, take the time to list out ten items you are grateful for. After listing out the ten items, read each item out loud and recite after each one, "Thank you from my heart." It is important to hear what you are creating. Why is gratitude so important? This is about your state of mind. A person who owns a way of thinking that is grateful does not have space for negative thinking. This is a practice which will make its difference with use.

R.E.C.C. Writing: Reasons, Excuses, Concerns, and Considerations

For this practice, you will choose one area of life, a choice you are facing or something you would like to see shift in your life. Write out all of your reasons, excuses, concerns, and considerations for this area of your life. Allow yourself no more than 30 minutes to complete this writing, and this may only take a few minutes. The last step to this process is the most important, the creation of something new. A declaration of something you are going to live.

1. Set a timer for 30 minutes.

2. Choose an area of life to work on.

3. Write out all the reasons, excuses, concerns, and considerations.

4. Rip up the paper and throw it away.

5. Create a declaration as a stand for your future.

6. "I declare I am_____ (strong, smart, wonderful, amazing)."

These tools are designed to give you a foundation for creating your life. The conversations of society, parents, and friends don't have to be the same conversations we have with ourselves. You can and you will create your life, one that is extraordinary and one that you deserve. Thank you for who you are, and all that you do.

CHAPTER

Twelve

Attracting Magic Through Mindful Alignment
By Kim Purcell

KIM PURCELL

Kim Purcell is a Wellness Warrior, wife, mother, sister, daughter, and friend. Married to her husband for nearly 18 years, they have three beautiful, healthy, thriving teenage children. Kim worked in trade publishing for nearly 15 years, in the fields of medical device and nutrition manufacturing. It was there that she developed her passion for nutrition. Diagnosed with Crohn's disease and Colitis over 20 years ago, Kim healed herself through food and nutrition. During the last 10 years, Kim has worked in the nutrition field, helping individuals establish their own small businesses. For the past 5 years, Kim has been working with women and teen girls on their own journeys toward wellness in Ponte Vedra Beach, Florida. While she jokes, she is more likely certifiable than certified, she would love to invite you into her huge loving heart, to help in any way she can. To reach her, call 904-545-1327 or agehealthier@gmail.com.

Acknowledgments

Special thanks to my friends, the authors of "Dreaming Heaven: the Journey Book", Lee McCormick, Gini Gentry, Francis Rico for your wisdom, support and teachings over the years, and to Kelly Sullivan Walden for giving birth to this book that has changed so many lives. Thank you also to my soul sister and partner, Dr. Cheralyn Leeby, Ph.D. LMFT for jumping in to co-lead the journeys with me. Thank you to Jorge Luis Delgado for sharing your wisdom and your teachings with me, and to all my teachers and mentors over the years who have helped me grow. Thank you mostly to my friends and family, especially to my lovely mother, Joanne Droge and my father, Dr Edward F. Droge, Jr., Ed.D., and my beautiful, hard working husband, Ken Purcell, and my darling children, Bryce, Darby and Parker for loving me through.

Attracting Magic Through Mindful Alignment
By Kim Purcell

Have you ever experienced times when life felt almost magical, when your thoughts and energy felt clear and light as if you were floating through your days without a worry or dark thought? Your heart was filled with peace and synchronicities abounded. You thought of a friend; the phone rang and there she was on the line. You wished for enough money to go somewhere, and a check surprisingly arrived in the mail. An invitation came to go somewhere you'd only dreamed of going. Those times feel surreal. You find yourself asking, "What great thing is going to happen next?"

For me, those times used to happen from time to time serendipitously. I tried to stay in them and float above my world on my magic cloud while greeting each magical moment and each great thing that landed in my lap. But eventually, those times would pass, and a long time might pass until those magical moments would cluster together again. What I have learned is that it doesn't have to be serendipity. It is possible to invite that magic into your life and stay there. Of course, we can't control everything that happens in our world, but there is a formula to getting to that place and a formula to make it last. It does take work, but hands-down, the work is worth it. The gift is freedom. What is possible is more than we ever thought it to be. We are more powerful than we've ever been told. Ultimately, the goal is to keep alignment with your mind, body, and soul.

Let's start with the mind. Sometimes, the thoughts in our head become our truth. Not because they're backed by science or proven in any way to be true, but as Don Miguel Ruiz points out, "We have made an agreement that they are true." They are true in our minds because we believe them to be. Over a lifetime, our beliefs color how we see the world; how we make decisions. For example, use the belief that men are superior to women. You may have been taught this belief by your family, then it was confirmed in society, and then cemented in your mind. If you were to question that belief, you might find evidence to the contrary. You might find sufficient evidence to turn that belief upside down and prove the opposite. That belief was born from a place of limitation, not from a place of truth. It was your perspective. When we step back, identify and question our beliefs, we begin to clear our lens, free from judgment.

Think about all the thoughts that go through your head consistently. They might sound like. "You are not smart enough, thin enough, tough enough, tall enough, athletic enough." The list can go on to include all the places you don't feel good enough. If you were to identify when each of your beliefs came to be, it would take some time, but it would be illuminating. Maybe your teacher called you stupid, or a coach said you would never make the team, or someone else ended up with your high school crush.

Somewhere along the line, those thoughts became beliefs and they shaded everything you thought to be possible for you in this lifetime, through a lens of "not good enough." The reality is, maybe that was true for that instant? Maybe, it was never true at all. Still, that belief was never questioned—until now. Take some time to write down a list of limiting thoughts and beliefs about yourself, of others, as well as, your morals and values. Take time to question each belief. Ask yourself when you first came to believe that. It can be important to determine when you first thought it, so it might shine a light on how or why it is limited. Next, ask if it is true. Chances are you might want to rethink some of those beliefs. The work is to become the witness to your mind. Separate the "you" who is thinking from the "you" who is listening. Start to become conscious of what you're thinking.

Most of us go through the day with so many thoughts running through our heads. We call this 'mind chatter' many things: mental noise, voices in our heads. Native Americans call this mind chatter "mitote." Neuroscientists say we only use one-tenth of our brain cells. Does that mean if we used more of our minds that we might come to see more clearly? I don't think so. If we were to look at the over seven billion people in the world, we would see over seven billion world views of religion, politics, success, failure, self-esteem and happy homes. The list goes on. It's beyond subjectivity. It means that there are over seven billion versions of reality on this planet because every person has their view. And, not even one of these is true. They are all limited by perspective.

We allow ourselves to be hooked by our minds all day long until our heads hit the pillow at night. Many thoughts are not even ours. They're preprogrammed by the world we live in, the family we grew up in, the media, even our ancestors. The key is that we are not our minds. We are the ones listening. The mind has its own operating system. You—the one who is listening to these thoughts, answering questions in your head—are in charge, not your mind. It's time to fire your mind and give it a demotion! It has been the boss of you long enough. It's time to change the operating software in your brain and release the thoughts in your head that stop you from living a free, purpose-filled life. Your spirit, your soul, your inner wisdom, we call that "you" a lot of different things. But, hardly do we call it "boss."

When we see the world from the viewpoint of the one who is listening, we empower ourselves. We can hear our thoughts and choose whether to act on them or let them float by without giving them our attention. By choosing where we put our attention, we tap into a power infinitely greater than we have allowed ourselves to believe we have. Most people don't see their thoughts as thoughts. Their thoughts tell them what to see and believe. When we see things the other way around, we move into our magic.

Science shows that there are biochemical changes that happen in the body when we are in love. The body is indisputably healthier when we are in that honeymoon phase of a relationship. So, it follows that the key to bringing back the magic in your body begins by falling in love—with your body. It might sound hard to imagine. But, it is a critical step to fall in love with the aspect of you that is your physical vehicle on this earth. If you've ever been in an intimate relationship with someone else, especially when you were young, you might remember sharing the story of every scar on your body with them. With kindness and even a bit of sadness, you relate the story of the injury that resulted in that mark. The first step of falling in love with your body is to see it exactly as it is. Stand in front of the mirror naked, and just notice. Notice with loving kindness and without judgment every part of you, every lump or bump or imperfection. Whether you like it or not at this moment is no matter. The work is to be able to stand in front of the mirror naked and tell yourself, "I love you." To do this fully, you might first need to make amends with your body.

Write a letter to your body. Apologize for all the ways you have wronged your physical body and express deep gratitude for it taking you this far in your life. After you have written the letter, take time to read it to yourself, and allow the conscious you to forgive yourself. That doesn't mean condoning every behavior you have done to your body; it only means with gentleness and compassion you no longer harbor any resentment toward yourself for those past wrongs. Set yourself free from the shame and blame of any way you may have been unkind or unloving to your body in the past. If any of these actions are still taking place, take time to make a vow to your body to stop misusing it, or abusing it. Make a vow from this point forward to love yourself, naked in front of the mirror. It should be a daily practice to stand in front of the mirror and tell yourself, "I love you." If it feels impossible at first, start by smiling at yourself in the mirror. Genuinely smile at yourself; greet yourself with kindness, and eventually, you can work up to love.

Once you have made amends with your body, it is time to write your eulogy. This exercise may seem maudlin, but it is not. The reality is we will all die someday. Some of the magic is to live each day as if it were our last. How might our days be different if they were numbered? Who might we forgive? To whom might we need to apologize? To whom might we show more love? Take time to journal those things. In writing your eulogy, imagine what you want your legacy to be. Ask yourself, are you living your legacy now? What might you change in how you act each day to be the person you want to be in your eulogy?

Now that your mind and body are lining up, let's talk about the soul and clarify the term. Soul is another term for who you are on a heart level: the conscious you, your spirit, your divine center. Maybe you call it your higher self? Whether you believe in one God, many gods, Mother Nature, the universe, all the above, or none of the above—it is no matter in this chapter. We do assume that our soul is connected to a larger universal soul or divine consciousness of some sort. I hope that with quantum physics and the entanglement theory being well-established that we can all agree that we are interconnected to every living thing. For our purpose, we will refer to that central connecting point as the soul. Imagine the soul as you would a child's picture of the sun.

When the soul is clear, well and thriving, the little rays that draw out from the center of the glowing ball of light, reach far out into the universe, to Mother Nature, the cosmos, to each other, to the heavens and beyond. But, if we are not in a consistent alignment practice, our energy can become heavy. Our souls become congested, unable to reach out limitlessly into the magical realm of infinite possibility. To unclog the blockages around our soul body, we must free ourselves from our past stories.

Imagine all your life's stories, in living detail, laid out on a massive open field. Imagine the conscious you, rising above the stories of your past, but tethered to each story as you rise, almost like the roots of a plant. As you rise above, become the witness. These are the stories of your past; they are not who you are. We carry our past on our shoulders like a weight. Envision yourself spanning out and cutting the cord that binds you to each story of your past, one by one. This may take hours, or it may take weeks. It is a process, and if your past is traumatic, you might want to have someone support you through this process. The work is to leave the suffering on the field. Detach yourself from the weight of your past. Watch yourself rise above each incident, defining moment, each trauma and each joy, noticing it is simply a blip in time. It is not who you are. Though the event may have been profoundly sad, disfiguring or devastating in some way, realize that the event itself is only a blip in time. While we can never change the past, we can change how we view that moment in time. We can choose to be anchored to that moment forever or operate from a free soul, formed by the moment, but no longer attached to it. With loving kindness, gently cut each cord and free your soul from its attachment to your past.

You've done the work. You have become the witness to your life, to your thoughts, and to your past. The doorway to our magic opens when we release our baggage fully, from our mind, body and our souls. Within your soul is the key to the magic within you, the magic that connects you to every living thing, to your purpose and to manifesting your deepest desires. Practice daily keeping that majestic soul doorway clear with your breath. The word *breathe* in Latin is, "spirare," and the word *spirit* in Latin is "spiratus." It is no mistake that these ancient people knew that one of the keys to connecting to the Holy Spirit or even your spirit is through the mindfulness tool of the breath. We can invite divine alignment with our minds, bodies and our souls at a moment's notice by using the breath. If you feel you are not operating from your true place of magical possibility, but instead from that old place of limitation, stop and breathe.

Breathe and become the witness. Return to the conscious "you," connected to the wisdom of your ancestors, and the collective wisdom that is your birthright. Pause and breathe in gently but fully; breathe in love, light and clarity, and breathe out anything that does not serve you in that moment with a forceful exhale if you can. Pffoooofff! Just like you are dusting off that magic wand with your out breath, release the mind chatter, the negative thoughts, the tension in your body, the haunting memories of your past. Let them all go. That is not who you are. You, my dear reader, are a mindful, masterful maker of magic. The power is yours.

The world is a kinder place when we are filled with kindness. It's the law of attraction. Look for signs to remind you that you are continuing in the right direction. These signs are everywhere when your vision is clear.

CHAPTER

Thirteen

The Expedition Of Self: Fullness Through Awareness And Acceptance
By Laura Rudacille

LAURA RUDACILLE

Laura Rudacille is a bestselling author, enrichment presenter, creator/facilitator of Awakening Goddess Retreats, project manager with Gyrlfriend Collective LLC, certified restorative and chair yoga practitioner, and premier member of the Women's Speakers Association. Thirty years in the salon industry has taught Laura the value of good listening and human connection. As women shared their experiences, a root of commonality was exposed. Inspired, Laura published her novel, *Invisible Woman*, and expanded her vision to include workshops and destination retreats uniting and encouraging women to celebrate every season of life. Her thought-partnering insight and candid humor sheds light on our similarities and infuses positivity and possibility into every moment. Connect with Laura at:

www.LauraRudacille.com

and on Facebook. Join the Conversation, Sunday evenings in her private group for women's enrichment the AGR Hen House.

Acknowledgments

The challenge and reward of writing is more meaningful thanks to the support of many. To Keith, my brother and champion, thank you for your steadfast faith and encouragement to embrace a blank page and offer fresh words. To my prayer and positivity partners: Laurie, Candi, Joni, Julie, Samantha, Tina, Nikki, Mindy, and Liz—thank you for every positive text, shared laugh, vulnerable tear, and loving edit. To Adam, my husband, and sons Mason and Teague—thanks for enduring creative cooking and computer frustration; I love you. To the As You Wish Publishing Team, especially my publisher, Kyra, you're goodness in abundance! Thank you for inviting me to this project and for bringing out the best in me. To the ladies of the AGR Hen House and women who demonstrate profound insight and authenticity ~ continue to celebrate who you are, and spill over into the world you walk in.

The Expedition Of Self:
Fullness Through Awareness
And Acceptance
By Laura Rudacille

"Gear up," I said to my client. "We're going to dig in and get dirty."

"The expedition of self is a journey I never wanted to go on," she said. "Seriously, I'm with me all day every day, so what's to discover?"

"Tons," I answered, "...and I mean *tons*. It's impossible to embrace the woman you're becoming unless you intend to become her."

You were designed on purpose, born whole, and created in God's perfect image. He knows who you are and is delighted in your strength and persevering heart. Wonderfully made, you have everything you need to fulfill your discovery of self. Through listening, connection, and community, you'll cultivate your love legacy, awaken awareness, and reinforce acceptance by focusing on the virtues of love stitched into every fiber of who you are.

Embrace love, reframe, and release limiting language and begin to pursue the miraculous possibility nestled within you. Transform your thoughts, and your heart will follow. It's an inside job and requires intentional heart-work, an inward dive to decipher restrictive beliefs which shorten your strides and hamper your growth and movement. I'm excited to encourage your enduring expedition of self—and make no mistake—it is an expedition. You need gear, intention, patience, and persistence.

Beginning in the Middle

You are where you are, and that's okay. For many, the pain of accepting responsibility for their starting point will prevent taking the first step toward healing fullness. You are where you are because of the choices you've made and circumstances you've experienced.

You may have wandered off course or were misdirected. In some cases, you linked your fingers with an offered hand and followed willingly. Perhaps you ran into the storm to escape and were unprepared for the exposure. Maybe you were tempted or teased by better or more thinking, your quest for independence was guided, and questions were posed. "What do you want to be?" shifted focus from who you are. Weary, disoriented, lost or abandoned, carrying burdens of unforgiveness, hurt or fear, you've arrived in the messy middle.

Parts of your heart have sought and found comfort in the shadows. Fullness is not a destination, but a horizon of decisions made repeatedly. You can't outsmart your healing. In the shadows, away from the noisy driven world, there is possibility to begin again.

Shift from the Shadow to the Shade

Shadows are for hiding; shade is for recovery. In this moment, be expectant as you decide to shift your thoughts and slide into the healing perspective of possibility. In the restorative shade, no longer contorting, camouflaging, or hiding in plain sight behind the mask of achievement, humor, or destructive behavior, you will open pathways to awareness and acceptance. This is an opportunity to discover (or rediscover) all you are uniquely designed to be. It's wiggly. It takes vulnerability, but you'd better believe it's worth it.

Championing your fullness begins with listening intently to yourself. Trust me, a lot is being said behind the scenes within your head and heart. I encourage you to get curious and love yourself enough to listen. The dialog in your head is a no-joke obstacle.

We all endure a constant stream of internal dialog, a filibuster of guidance even when we're at rest. I affectionately call the two resident influencers the WIOH and the SOUL sister.

WIOH = (witch-in-our-head); SOUL = (supportive, optimistic, understanding, loving)

Both your WIOH and your SOUL sister aspire to support and your living fullness; however, the origins of their guidance and the tones of their delivery are vastly different.

Your WIOH has seen it all, been affected, and remembers everything. From your first breath, she's formed opinions, passed legislation, and erected walls of protection. Although her motives are rooted in safety, her rules and actions were formed in the moment with the reason and knowledge her age offered. Survival and coping skills learned at a vulnerable age establish patterns which are carried for years. Accustomed to theses split-second verbal, physical and emotional reactions, you may have never considered questioning if the advice fits the woman you are in this moment.

Your SOUL sister will not compete for the stage or rip the microphone from the WIOH's hand, but she would love to offer a fresh point of view. I encourage you to infuse her supportive, optimistic, understanding, loving perspective.

Cultivating an intentional, loving response is developed at the Truth Table with an unearthing process I call the Why Dive. Gather around the Truth Table and welcome space for healing and growth. Invite self-awareness to redefine perceived truth and usher in a new pattern of thinking.

A Why Dive gets to the root of the WIOH's dusty hurts and limiting language, so you may apply the SOUL sister's reason and wisdom. Give yourself the transformative opportunity to discover, reframe, and release outgrown reactive response.

Shift into the discovery process and embrace vulnerability with gentleness. The Truth Table is a safe place, where scorching scrutiny, outside opinion, and influence have no say. Investigate individualized thought patterns and reactive responses. Notice language, behavior, and relationships, which evoke an instinctive, intuitive, and visceral reaction within you. Draw awareness to instances that trigger you to shrink or withdraw, as well as situations that insight anger, fear or comfort: food, sex, binge behaviors, or even exercise.

In the light of day, your vulnerability, unexpected exposures, or sneak attacks on your becoming process can be viewed with fresh perspective. In the safe space of this present moment, revisit the origin of your reaction. How old were you? Where were you and with whom? The key to your release lies in recognition of your present.

As you analyze knee-jerk flashes, revisit your abundant store of wired-in love. If a bubbling WIOH response urges you wield your finger to point out fault or proclaim justification of hurt, I encourage you to turn your accusing finger toward yourself. You have the power in this moment to stop assigning blame and claim your right to move in your way with the skills and knowledge of today. Be brave enough to distinguish present truth over outgrown ideas within your inner dialog. You are beyond impact, and clear of exposure. You are strong.

Release and Welcome Drainage

My friend Candi has a knack for keeping houseplants alive, a skill I lack. She shared that an important and often overlooked key to thriving potted plant life is drainage. Not more sun, water, or special fixes from the gardening supply store—drainage.

There is freedom in releasing your grip on habitual reaction. Stepping away from undernourished relationships and situations opens space for healthy growing and may enrich the soil, cultivating a new pathway to fullness.

Your SOUL sister is ready to support your drainage. She's ready to champion intentional unburdening as you redefine every word of mass destruction your WIOH mutters. Chip away at any language that no longer fits. Fluid healing begins with a shift in perspective. If you're clenching dusty hurt, invite the swell of sadness, allow it to leak from your eyes, and breathe away any tightness in your heart.

Welcome transformation and heart-centered fullness from the inside out as your SOUL sister encourages your grip to loosen. Open your drain and release cycles of comfort, limiting language, and auto-responses that are not for you any longer. Release your fingers and marvel at the breathing room. Lead with grace, forgiveness, and laughter as you grow into your hollow spaces and shift into all you are becoming.

Provide room for your SOUL sister's language to strengthen. Celebrate every new syllable of support, optimism, understating, and love. Offer buckets of compassionate understanding to the girl you once were. Delight in the opportunity for fullness as the gifts of enrichment arrive. Shift from the shadow to the shade, and as you are ready, slide on a pair of sunglasses and step into the sun, armed with the wisdom of your present truth.

Strength in Until

My greatest revelations happen in the quiet between twilight and daybreak as I drift amid wake and sleep, the stirring of my still, small voice of knowing whispers. Connection in the stillness reminds me of the wholeness and possibility sown in at birth.

I spent my mid-twenties hiding in plain sight. Armed with humor and brash confidence, my pursuit of fullness had resulted in perceived isolation and loneliness. Unfulfilled and anxious, I began a practice of intentional positivity to calm my heart every night. I repeated a prayerful mantra as I drifted to sleep. I used three words for what I was desperately seeking: peace, patience, and understanding.

During this unsettled season, I pleaded for a rewind to undo my cleverness, an appeal to heal the brokenness hidden within my poised and painted smile. My simple practice, clumsy at first, proved to be the proper footwear for navigating the unpredictable terrain. Over time, ease and softening provided stability and comfort for the unseen miles ahead.

"You do all things, until you know better."

As you move through awareness and acceptance, be reminded that you were born whole. The light in you wants to be seen, and the light you seek desires your presence. New ways of thinking may make us wiggly, but an individual with focus has purpose and an individual with purpose has hope. Today you can be your hero. Release any fuss, complacency, excuses, and decide to embrace possibility.

You're in the process of becoming. It's an ongoing personal investment, not an overnight success, buy-with-one-click rush to perfection, but a patient, persistent, discovery of self. I encourage you to love yourself too much to stay where you are.

"You have more power than you know."

Investigate your hollow spaces. Void of mindless eating, at-all-cost achievement, or impulse shopping, the openness may feel like exposure. Stand in it. (Mountain pose: feet firmly planted, the crown of the head lifted, spine aligned, shoulder blades back and down.) Stand in balance, power, and patience, until.

"Until is my favorite two syllable possibility on the path to becoming."

Today, this moment, your "until" has arrived. Pause and glance over your shoulder. No longer wishing in a fabled rewind, rejoice the miracle of how far you've come. Celebrate how much you have learned. Stretch your arms wide and turn slowly in a wide circle as you soak in the view. Every day the world offers vibrant color to delight your eyes, aroma to flood your senses, music to elevate your mood, and you, a thing within the things, are encouraged to dance.

Connect, Conspire, Collaborate

I've worked in the salon industry for over thirty years and witnessed decades of frontline exposure as women navigated the unpredictably of life. Enduring, triumphant, warriors, they celebrated as they rediscovered themselves by casualty and by choice. I marveled as even in adversity they wore vulnerability with inspiring influence. Their example taught me strength and perseverance beyond measure.

One of the most vital and empowering pearls of wisdom ever imparted to me was, "Be who you're looking for." Exude what you are seeking, and your expedition will be joined by those who share your heart's longing for fullness through heart-centered intentional positivity and love. Be the first one to the party and dance. Twirl, shimmy, gyrate, and in a blink, your dance floor will be delightfully crowded. Your expedition will lead you to action as you heal and embrace your wholeness. Your breakthrough will come in an easy smile, a gentle word, a spine straightening moment of self-preservation or confidence.

Embrace the Unfolding

The demands of society may urge you to set aside pieces of who you are in a rush to go further, faster. Exposure and impacts may scuff your comfy boots, and in defense, you'll pull on additional layers of protection.

Sit a bit. Unlace your boots, strip off your socks and wiggle your toes. Welcome a moment of rest to gain perspective. Wait in the quiet stillness with faithful obedience. Your present decisions are paving the way for spiraling waves of goodness.

Liberate your heart with love. Loosen your grip. Allow your fingers to unfold and your palms to open to the possibility. Release dusty hurts, limiting relationships, and outgrown reactive comfort. Discharge every anxiety, worry, and obsessive thought threatening to swallow you, and with renewed confidence, outgrown barriers to your fullness crumble.

Faith released is more powerfully than any perceived limitation. Restore and embrace the unfolding. Trust your still small voice of knowing. God is at work on the front line and behind the scenes. Listen, receive, until.

Expanded Exploration:

1. What qualities do you admire most in others? List three ways you may begin to cultivate these in yourself.

2. Visit the Truth Table and Why Dive limiting language and reaction responses. Redefine and release using the SOUL sister's voice.

3. Develop a prayerful mantra. Choose three words of intention and repeat them in stillness for three to five minutes, or as you fall asleep.

4. Awareness Exercise: Stand in mountain pose. As breath moves in and out, observe your posture from soles of feet, to the crown of the head.

Legacy of Love Guided Meditation

The virtues of love surround us in abundance every day: kindness, understanding, strength of self-control, patience, endurance, and forgiveness. Designed in and for the love we're intended to cultivate an ongoing supply, so we may live in fullness and spill over into our homes and community in a beautiful spiral of expanding goodness.

What do you want your love legacy to say about you? Are you nurturing yourself on purpose? Be encouraged and begin with the virtue of Kindness.

In this moment, smile. Allow the movement of your cheeks to lift your spirit and ease your busy mind. Breathe into your smile, giving it kindness, life, and movement. Offer your smile to another person in your home, on the sidewalk, or in the grocery store. Allow the exchange to fill you with goodness.

Floating on the wave of kindness, recall a moment of understanding, strength of self-control, patience, endurance or forgiveness, and actively grow your supply of the abundant virtues of love. Envision what love feels like to you, what love looks like to you, what love sounds and smells like to you. Imagine the sun's warmth on your face. Inhale the aroma of your favorite flower. Rise with the swell of a melody or tap your toes with a pulse-racing rhythm. Becoming whole through love offers a powerful possibility to rediscover all you are.

Grow, develop, and build upon the virtues of love and live in fullness. Cultivate life-giving virtues of love and spill over into your home and community in a spiral of expanding goodness. Love, for you from you. Love from you to others.

CHAPTER

Fourteen

If I Were Brave
By Linda Ballesteros

LINDA BALLESTEROS

As a Certified Franchise Broker, Linda Ballesteros taps into her over 30 years in the banking industry as well as her coaching background to support and guide her clients. Her unique approach to match clients is achieved by finding the up and coming franchise that is best suited for each client's individual passion and skills. This allows her to empower those seeking to build a solid financial future and leave a legacy through business ownership. You can also hear Linda's interview skills on one of the many radio shows she has hosted over the years.

Contact Info:

www.mpowerfranchiseconsulting.com
Linda@mpowerfranchiseconsulting.com
www.facebook.com/MpowerFranchiseConsulting/
www.facebook.com/AllThingsFranchising/
www.linkedin.com/in/lindaballesteros/
832-640-4922

Acknowledgments

My Mario (soulmate), April Chalk (daughter), Justin Keppinger (son-in-law), Marty and Teresa Ballesteros (brother-in-law and sister-in-law), Members of University Heights Church in Huntsville, TX (amazing loving and supportive congregation), Tony and Wendy Gambone (dear friends who opened their home and hearts to us), Joyce Owen (sister), Leon Jeffcoat (brother), Charlie and Norma Jeffcoat (brother and sister-in-law), Keri Shaw (long-time soul sister), Elizabeth Harbin (long-time soul sister), Eleanor Rhodes (spirit mother), Dr. Barry Morguelan (teacher), Judy Morris (friend), Cindy Childress (new friend).

If I Were Brave
By Linda Ballesteros

Have you ever experienced an event that changed your life forever? That's what happened to me when the love of my life, my partner in crime, business partner, dance partner, and husband lost his battle with cancer in 2016.

I have generally been a brave woman. Until my Mario became ill, I thought the bravest thing I'd ever done was walk away from my successful career in banking. I made the decision to quit when the security badge I put around my neck every morning became heavier, almost like a ball and chain, when finally, I told my boss I was leaving.

"Are you going to a rival bank?" he asked.

"No way!" I exclaimed.

"Did a customer lure you away?"

"Not that, either."

"Well, what are you going to do then?"

"I have no idea, but it has to be more purposeful."

I walked out of the bank that day with no plan of what I was going to do to replace my income or benefits. All I knew was that I was not living in alignment with my life's purpose even though I had not pinpointed what that was.

After leaving my more than 30-year career in banking, I began learning about myself, my hidden strengths, untapped talents and being an entrepreneur. I tried to live my life in tune with my intuition and in alignment with what felt like my purpose. That's why being a life coach and working with women who want to leave corporate jobs and own franchise businesses is a natural fit for me.

Years later, I would come to realize that leaving corporate was not the bravest thing I had ever done. My bravest moments arose when I became a caregiver for Mario, and I had to make bold decisions every day. I didn't feel brave at all. I felt like I was treading water and trying to keep afloat.

During these challenging and sometimes unbearable days of being a caregiver, I had to lean heavily on my beliefs and dig deeply into my training as a life coach. I had to shift the way I approached this crisis because it was like nothing I had experienced before. I had to be vulnerable and open to making space for miracles. I had to turn to my support system, and most importantly, I had to go with my gut.

I built a Bravery Tool Kit along the way and will be sharing some of those tools throughout for you to use where and when you might find them beneficial.

Be Vulnerable to Make Room for Miracles

Mario was a successful CPA/CFO and was well respected in the Houston business community. He mentored financial executives and assisted in advancing their careers. Mario had a servant's heart and a giving attitude which takes confidence and vulnerability.

I remember when we met in dance class and we were two-stepping around the dance floor. He tossed his head back and said, "If only I were 6'2" instead of so devilishly good-looking." You see, he was two inches shorter than me. That was when I discovered there is nothing more attractive than a man who is not afraid to show his vulnerable side. This became the foundation of our marriage, and we supported and encouraged each other to live our best lives.

Mario's health started failing about ten years into our marriage. Both of our worlds were about to change drastically. To say he was brilliant when it came to answers and research is an understatement. Now, it fell on my shoulders because my Mario was becoming less effective in the areas he loved so much. I now had to become the strong one. One morning, I could see he was becoming weaker, and in a private moment I said, "I can't do this by myself anymore." I surrendered to a higher power. I had done all I could do alone. The next day, I received a call from dear friends who invited us to stay with them and get a second opinion. It was then that I realized what surrender meant and what a difference it could make.

I was overwhelmed with emotion and felt that my cry for help had been heard, and my prayers were answered. We graciously accepted their generosity. Sadly, the second opinions did not change the prognosis. In fact, the harsh reality that he would never twirl me around the dance floor again set in. Mario was facing the final act of vulnerability by living out his last 19 days at his brother's home in hospice. Looking back on those final days, I realize I could never have cared for him without the help of my brother-in-law and sister-in-law. We became a team and approached Mario's care with the sole purpose of creating a safe environment for him to make his transition. At no time during those 19 days did I feel brave. In fact, I tried not to feel anything because it was too painful.

The three of us were by his side when he took his last breath on Memorial Day, May 30, 2016. This was especially appropriate because he was proud to say that he served his country in the United States Air Force.

Somehow, I had to continue to move forward and build a life without a partner. This was not the life I created on my vision boards. However, it was my new reality. I had to put one foot in front of the other and keep breathing. I sold most of our things, put the rest of my belongings in storage and gave myself three months to visit friends and try to find myself again in this new life.

Even though Houston is my home, I could not bear to live there without Mario. It was where we grew up and where the dance studio was located that revealed our mutual love for music and dance. Our family and friends were close. We had a huge business networking community that knew us as a "power couple." You might think this would give me comfort in some way; however, I couldn't see myself there without him. I needed not only a fresh start, but I also needed to prove to myself that I could do it alone.

Bravery Tool Kit #1

In the crises of caregiving, I realized that my normal approach to prayer and affirmations wouldn't cut it. Instead of saying, "I am brave," I would say, "I can be brave in this moment." Speaking them out loud and writing my affirmations a hundred times over seemed to supercharge the intention.

You can do the same thing. Think about a challenge you're facing now. Are you willing to admit that you don't have all the answers and are open to receiving help? Create an affirmation and flood your brain with it multiple times a day to open yourself to blessings beyond your imagination.

Find Meaning Through Your Challenges

By again opening space for new possibilities, a path emerged for me to move to Dallas where my old friend, Elizabeth, was caring for her mother who eventually went into hospice care.

While I was helping Elizabeth care for her mother, I processed the painful memories of what I had just gone through. One of the most difficult shifts for me was to realize that Mario's journey was between himself and God, and I didn't get a vote. As a caregiver, that is one of the hardest things to accept. I recognized when Elizabeth's mother was at that point, and I was able to support my friend to accept the inevitable life change that was coming. I also knew with 100% certainty that I was where I was supposed to be and was doing what I was supposed to do in alignment with my soul's purpose. I was living the life of purpose that I had left banking to seek.

Bravery Tool Kit #2

Challenges don't always have to be this dramatic. Look at past challenges you have faced in your personal life and business. List at least five to seven of them. Circle the ones whose meaning you feel you understand as well as the ones where you've served others because of your experience.

Use tools to help calm your mind if there's a lot of emotional charge on an issue. I used binaural code music, Emotional Freedom Technique (EFT), meditation and any other resources I could find. Using these tools allowed meaning and purpose to emerge quickly.

Go with Your Gut

Bravery doesn't mean that you're never afraid—it means that you're afraid but you move forward anyway, even in the scariest moments. To do so, you must align yourself with your intuition and use your inner truth to guide you through the hard times.

Being a caregiver means you are always "on." Hypersensitive listening at doctors' appointments and taking notes are critical to be an informed caregiver. It's scary to think you have that much responsibility for another person's life. I would struggle to ensure I received all of the information from the doctors, and we followed it to the smallest detail. But, even then I had to stay checked-in with my gut to follow my intuition.

Early in his treatment, Mario's oncologist suggested a clinical trial drug, and I had already researched this drug. I froze at the suggestion because, from what I'd read, this drug had fatal side effects my husband would never survive. I could have assumed the doctor knew best and quieted the voice inside me, but I didn't. I reminded the doctor that Mario also had Congestive Heart Failure and that drug strains the heart. "Is this really the right drug?" I asked. I could see that the doctor's mind was whirling, and he stepped out of the room for a moment.

He came back and said, "That's a good question. He can't be on that drug." Speaking out when you're in the medical system can be tough, but your brain and intuition must always be present in a crisis.

Another way to plug into your intuition is to stay in the present and focus narrowly on what's right in front of you to move forward.

I think of it like this:

- Focusing on the future creates anxiety.

- Focusing on the past causes depression.

- That is why we must stay in the present.

Taking care of Mario, I could second-guess myself about the choices of doctors, but I had to lean heavily on my faith that I was going to be given the information I needed, and the right people would appear. If I played a "what if" game, I would always feel like I didn't do enough, but focusing on the present, I knew I was doing everything I could with the information I had.

If I tried to look too far down the road, I didn't have all the information to make those decisions and would feel overwhelmed. Things change quickly in a crisis and trying to decide something today for next month is unrealistic, so I did my best to look at the task at hand.

Bravery Tool Kit #3

You can't always know everything about every moving part or personally handle everything, but you also must keep going and get the information you need to get to the next step.

Here's my best way to stay persistent: trust your hunches, and look at the path in front of you and where to put your foot for the next step, metaphorically speaking. Think of a struggle that feels impossible, and then take the following actions to gain traction and regain your higher vibrations.

1. Be curious: What don't you know about this issue that's bugging you? Who might have that information, and how can you get it? What's one thing you can do now to understand better what you're facing?

2. Notice how it feels: Are you stopping yourself from speaking up and stifling your truth? Do you feel worried? Are those worries logical and about the present, or are they stuck in the past or in the imaginary future?

3. Where are you right now: Define your present so that you can fully show up. What happened in the past that's no longer relevant or true? Knowing that allows you to release those stories that no longer serve you. What are you thinking about which is in the future and hasn't happened yet? Trim those thoughts away to see what's left at this moment, and then put your foot forward and take that next step.

Bravery requires you to be tough when you are faced with scary or difficult situations. No matter where you might be now in dealing with a tough situation, it's crucial that you continue to move forward. The same tools that applied in the major life events I have shared can also be applied in professional and career situations.

Let me give you an example of how, as a franchise broker, I guide my clients to use the tools I have shared with you today.

A corporate executive who had been downsized one time too many came to me to explore the idea of owning a franchise. He had researched well-known brands thinking that would give him instant success; however, they are pricey and a lot of work. Working with a franchise client is an intuitive process that works best when we take things one step at a time.

Once I was able to redirect his focus from missing his old co-workers and searching to replace the status his executive position gave him, we were able to move forward. As his goal became better defined, he trusted himself to make a well-informed and wise decision. We interviewed more than a half dozen franchise concepts. With each one, his questions became clearer, giving him the ability to hone in on what was important to him.

He is now the owner of a franchise which allows him the flexibility and the unlimited income potential that a corporate position could not. This is his first step in not only supporting his family but also building a legacy to leave for his family.

No matter where you might be now in dealing with a tough situation, it's crucial that you continue to move forward. Use the Bravery Tool Kit to create the space for miracles to happen, find meaning through your challenges, and go with your gut.

By refusing to listen to the voice of fear, I allowed the voice of bravery to whisper in my ear.

Today, you might be saying, "If I were brave..." and someday you may look back, as I do, and say, "I *am* brave!" *"The real man smiles in trouble, gathers strength from distress and grows brave by reflection."*—Thomas Paine

CHAPTER

Fifteen

Shame Off You
By Liz Reihm

LIZ REIHM

Liz believes that a "life fully lived" is possible for everyone and guides each client in discovering and embracing their full redemptive potential. Liz's practice, Coaching H.E.R., combines her experience as a life coach, nutrition consultant, and personal trainer to partner with women on their journey towards whole-body wellness. Liz designs personalized goal-oriented and solution-focused programs to address her clients' physical, emotional, and spiritual care. Liz holds a bachelor's degree in biblical studies and master's degree in professional counseling. She is also a board-certified Master Christian Life Coach. Before establishing her coaching business, Liz combined three of her greatest passions: fitness, traveling, and helping others create fulfilling lives, by teaching and counseling internationally. Liz believes it is a combination of her unique experience and a daily dose of God's grace that enables her to help women learn to live: Healthy, Empowered and Redeemed. For more information about local and virtual coaching services, contact Liz at www.coaching4her.com or liz@coaching4her.com

Acknowledgments

This writing project would not have happened without four important people in my life. The first being my incredibly supportive husband. His passion for life is contagious and his love empowers me to be the best version of myself and to chase down my dreams. He is one of the best writers I know, and I am so grateful for his suggestions and editorial contributions to my projects. I cannot thank my parents enough for their unconditional love and encouragement. They support every endeavor I take on, cheering for me with passion and confidence, emboldening me to take risks and go all in! My relationship with God is the foundation on which my life is built. Though I wandered and strayed along the way, this anchor establishes my true purpose for life. I've learned that the fullest expression of my life occurs when I love God and love others.

Shame Off You
By Liz Reihm

The first time I remember feeling it was when my childhood friend, Johnny, and I sat on the couch in his living room with our heads bowed, our eyes boring holes into the ground while our parents stood in the other room frantically discussing how to handle our little "indiscretion." The feeling spread throughout my entire body causing me to feel afraid, dirty, and wrong. Though I didn't know its name then, this unwelcomed guest made its introduction into my life with the plan to take off his coat and stay awhile. My little six-year-old mind was unaware of the intruder about to take up residence and cause a lot of disruption and pain throughout the next 30 years of my life. His name is Shame and boy did he make a mess of my house.

Shame is the thick blanket of contempt that shrouds us in feelings of humiliation, hopelessness, and regret. It calls us a failure and tells us we should run away, hide, and reject love from others because we are undeserving and unworthy. Guilt raises the alarm that I've done something wrong or made a mistake. Shame says, "I am wrong." "I am a mistake." Shame attacks our identity and takes our self-esteem hostage. When viewing myself through the unhealthy lens of shame, I unknowingly set myself up as a victim who simultaneously desired affection and isolation from others. When someone threatened the barriers I'd established to protect myself, withdrawal and isolation overrode the need for affection.

A fear of rejection combined with a desperate need to be loved often drove me towards behaviors offering immediate pleasure and avoidance of pain. My shame narrative started at six years old and evolved with each mistake I made. The negative self-talk became so sophisticated that it deceptively led me through life without consideration of an alternate reality. I became so accustomed to shame calling the shots I didn't even realize I had been hijacked. This is because shame masquerades as many other feelings. It hides in false beliefs, lies and dysfunctional perspectives and reactions, masking the imposter it is.

Just as our vehicles come equipped with indicators to alert us of malfunctions, our bodies are equipped with warning signals that notify us when we are not functioning at full capacity. Physically, this can appear as illness, pain, or diminished performance. Emotionally, it may manifest as depression, anxiety, fear, anger, and sadness. Feeling separation from God, dissatisfaction, a lack of peace, or emptiness often indicate spiritual impairment. Allowing the broken parts of our lives to dictate our thoughts, actions, and beliefs creates broken people and broken relationships. Like toddlers, ignoring these signs will not make them go away, they'll just get louder until you finally address them.

So, by now you may be wondering, if shame has the power to deceive and disable us (often unbeknownst to us), how do we address the patterns of dysfunction created by its inaccurate narrative running through our minds? How do we rewrite negative self-talk and false beliefs about who we are or our core value and worth?

As with any illness, healing begins with correctly identifying the problem. While shame is a part of all our stories on some level, each of us experiences different contributing factors and varying degrees of impact. Maybe you have been told by a loved one that you are unworthy. Perhaps someone reading this believes that what you've done in your past is unforgivable and makes redemption impossible. It's possible that your thoughts have held you captive for so long that you're just now realizing much of what you believe about yourself is a narrative created by shame and lies. If an uncomfortable sensation is rising in your chest right now as you think about the narrative that has come to define you, it could be your warning indicator notifying you that something is amiss. It is the first step towards recognizing and rewriting your shame story.

To become whole, we must first become aware of our brokenness. We cannot desire healing if we don't know we need it. And if we want to be whole, we need to be healed. Wholeness implies that we are complete, balanced, not lacking. It is functioning in the fullest expression of who we are designed to be. Wouldn't you love to begin living out the fullest expression of who you are in the life you are meant to have? If so, this is your time to make changes and start mending the holes preventing your wholeness.

I want to warn you that while healing and wholeness are possible for you, this process isn't fast or easy. It requires honest self-appraisal, which can be messy and painful. However, if you approach these steps with openness and vulnerability and commit to the necessary work, a new narrative of grace instead of shame and acceptance instead of rejection awaits you!

The following steps are a simple format to guide you through the process of change. I recommend that you find someone to walk this journey with you. That could be a professional life coach or counselor, a spiritual leader or pastor, or a trusted friend. I suggest this because of the emotional depth that surrounds our shame. A caring and objective perspective can help correct our subjective view of ourselves and circumstances (remember the thing we're addressing has likely been deceiving us most of our lives).

Three steps to rewrite our story:

1. Identify our illness
2. Initiate treatment
3. Internalize the change

Identify the Illness

To correctly identify the problem, we need to determine the source(s) of our shame and subsequent feelings. This begins with asking if your shame is rooted in something you did wrong or something wrong that was done to you? When do you first remember experiencing shame? Was a statement made about a mistake that caused you to feel worthless, dirty, or hopeless? Are there unrealistic expectations you've created or been subject to?

We must bring these deep-seated beliefs to light. Ignoring an illness does not make it go away. Denial only allows it to grow and fester. The same is true for shame. When we stuff it or try to hide the things we've done or from what's been done to us, we offer cover for the infection to grow. Darkness is exposed when we shine light on it. Shame is exposed when we shine truth on it. Once the source has been determined, it's time to go deeper.

Strategies to help identify the illness:

Ask: What are the predominant negative thoughts and feelings I have towards/about myself?

The root of shameful feelings most often stem from a belief we should have known better or that we should be able to do or not do a certain behavior/habit/activity. We tend to place expectations on ourselves and then feel shame when we don't live up to them.

Ask: What "Shoulds" and "Shouldn'ts" do I tell myself? Finish the sentence with your words:

I should be able to do
I should be strong enough to
I shouldn't let bother me
I shouldn't keep doing
I should know better than by now
I should be able to say no to
I shouldn't give into any more
I shouldn't need help with I'm so weak
I should be beyond this! Why does still impact/get the best of me
I should be able to keep my house clean
I should be able to get up and exercise every day
I should be a better (parent, friend, sibling, spouse...)
I should

Consider: The feelings that accompany thoughts of shame. When you think about who you are at the core or things you've done, these feelings often make you want to run or hide. Common descriptions: broken, despicable, dirty, hopeless, grief/sadness, never good enough, regret, resentful, self-contempt, self-pity, unworthy of forgiveness, unworthy of love.

Observe: Once you've identified the feelings you hold about yourself, observe the behaviors you engage in when you feel/think this way. Notice your default actions and responses when things get tough.

Common responses: addictions, comparison, control (self, others, or circumstances), escape (substance use, entertainment, sex, shopping, eating, exercise), isolate, lashing out, negative self-talk, reject love from others, self-harm, self-sabotage, withdrawal.

Initiate Treatment

Now that you have identified shame-induced illness in your life, you can begin treating the dysfunctional beliefs and behaviors. The false perceptions we create about ourselves do not develop overnight and will not be corrected or replaced immediately. The treatment process may require addressing more than one area of dysfunctional thinking. This could be repeated in a sequential format, addressing one concern after the other, or you may find that it occurs sporadically as new awareness arises around a negative root thought/belief. The key is to initiate treatment as soon as the problem is identified to begin the healing process.

Strategies to help initiate change:

Ask: Which negative belief, behavior, or "should" am I willing to confront right now?
Consider: Which treatment strategy best addresses this dysfunctional belief/behavior?
Accept difficult truths
Accept personal limitations (replace a 'should' with a 'can')
Challenge false beliefs
Embrace grace and self-compassion
Forgive yourself or others (daily as needed)
Journal about your triggers and new behaviors
Make amends
Pray for help in weakness
Replace destructive/dysfunctional behaviors with a positive action**
Replace negative self-talk with a positive truth**

Trigger Tracker
Write a 'let it go' letter to yourself from the perspective of unconditional love, acceptance, and forgiveness
***Use scripture/motivational quote visualization & memorization, ask a trusted friend for ideas, write out the negative belief in its opposite form, research healthy/positive activities to try, create a schedule to implement new behaviors, verbally repeat (yes, out loud) your new statement throughout the day, get professional treatment for addictions.

Observe: How are you responding to the treatment? Track how many times each day you replace the problem with the intervention strategy. What helped you? What hindered you? Where are you struggling the most with implementation? Do you need outside help or does a new approach need to be considered?

Internalize the Change

Behavior modification is great for just that—modifying behavior. However, if we do not internalize the change, get it down into the depths of our beings, the change will only be temporary. The treatment strategies listed above are just the starting point. As we continue to implement and integrate them into our thoughts and actions, we rewrite our inner narrative, and it becomes a part of us. Our thoughts become our beliefs, our beliefs dictate our behavior, our behaviors create habits, and our habits determine our character. Our character is who we truly are at the core of each of us. It is the person we are when nobody's looking, and it has the greatest impact on how we relate to ourselves and to others. When we love ourselves, we are more loving towards others. When we carry around self-contempt, we inevitably project it onto others. We cannot truly love others if we are unable to see ourselves worthy of love.

Strategies to help internalize the change:

Accept redemption
Embrace grace
Communicate Change

I'd like to say my struggle with shame ended as abruptly as it started, but that was not the case. It has taken over 30 years for me to fully understand and apply these principles to the destructive narrative that grew in volume with every mistake, failure, and poor choice I made. As a teenager, this struggle rarely entered my consciousness. In fact, I thought I was pretty great. Yet, as an adult, I now see that it just wasn't apparent to me at the time because I was working so hard to please everyone and live up to my own expectations. I didn't feel the shame because I was running so fast and so hard. It wasn't until I fell that I finally saw it. And, I fell hard! You see, all the accomplishments and praise and expectations I worked so hard to achieve throughout my teenage years only built a higher platform to fall from. And friends, I didn't just fall to the ground. I plummeted so hard, I created a deep, cavernous pit.

I found myself in the lowest part of this pit on May 3, 2012, when I got the call from the police officer who had just found my husband's body in the hotel room he was living in. He chose to end his life because, in his words, he could no longer stand the pain he had caused so many people and the hell he had put me through. Crushed by the weight of all our bad choices, the demise of our marriage, and now the ending of my husband's life. I laid in the depth of my pit and sobbed. Sobbed for my husband, for my failures, all I had lost, and all that could have been if we had stayed connected to God, our life source, in our hard times rather than trying to do it by ourselves.

It took about a year for me to climb out of the pit I had created. After the catastrophic mess I had made of my life, I didn't know how to embrace the unconditional love and grace I had learned about as a child. I remembered in the story called "The Prodigal Son" where the son cries out to his father, "I have sinned against you and God and I am not worthy to be called your child." That was exactly how I felt! Unworthy, a failure, regretful. Shame! I walked around subconsciously loathing myself as if my self-contempt would somehow cleanse me of my sins. But, it wasn't until I recognized my shame for what it really was that I finally confronted the lies I believed. I would be remiss if I didn't share with you how this happened. I was able to get by because I was a pro at behavior modification. However, it was not until I allowed the internal changes to take root in my heart through an acceptance of God's unconditional love and grace, that I was able to forgive myself. The understanding that I am fully loved despite my performance allowed me to accept redemption for my past, so I could fully embrace my present. Internalizing this truth meant replacing negative beliefs about myself with the truth of who my creator says I am. The act of internalizing the external changes breaks the narrative of shame that tells us, I'm not good enough or I have to be perfect to be acceptable.

This process is challenging work. It requires us to confront deep-seated lies of our shame and release the unrealistic expectations of our "shoulds." It takes discipline to rewrite our internal narrative and replace negative patterns. But we're not meant to limp through life just getting by. We're created to live out our fullest expression. Embracing these changes frees us from the bondage of perfectionism, apathy, and shame. It paves the way for our new identity to confidently say, "Shame off you!"

CHAPTER

Sixteen

Your Wellness Circle
By Mindy Quesenberry

MINDY QUESENBERRY

A life lived in her evolving "wellness circle," Mindy exercises mind, body, and soul to capture the essence of magic held within each of us. A heart for people, a passion for wellness, and the faith of God's purpose, she stands in her story of truth to connect with others. With years in the mental health field and a long career as a personal trainer, Mindy established her role as a movement motivator. The owner of F.I.T. Club powered by My Fitness Quest, and WPMT Fox43's wellness expert, she has entered the hearts of clients and viewers, sharing her knowledge and passion in weekly television segments "Wellness Wednesdays" and "Be Well Fridays." Mindy is on a mission to

bring light to others, inspiring them to find their joy, magic, and fulfillment to complete their "wellness circle."
www.fitclubyork.com
717-900-4132
mindy@ques-t.com

Acknowledgments

My heart is full through the love and support of my people. I praise you Lord, the glue, solidifying my truth, living well through you. To my sunshine, Ryder, you make me brave, believing I'm capable of anything. My love, BQ, when I'm down and done, you hold me up in love. Thank you, "Aubrey," together rescued and renewed. I honor my friends and family. Your prayers and words of encouragement always came when needed. High-fives F.I.T. Clubbers and Team Awesome. You "lift me higher", I'm honored to be in your wellness circle. Laura, my faithful friend and mentor, through you my voice is revealed on paper. Beyond blessed by your love and support. Liz, thank you for your light and for seeing me fully through this experience. Sue, my grounding guru, thank you for keeping me focused. To Kyra Schaefer and As You Wish Publishing, thanks for this opportunity to share my heart, a dream fulfilled. I'm blessed beyond measure, thank you.

Your Wellness Circle
By Mindy Quesenberry

A Call for Connection

To be well, or not to be well; you get to decide. Why stay in the ease of comfort or paralyzing fear when you can embrace reinvention through your reveal? Is it time to decide you're worthy of wellness? Wellness that comes with the conscious decision to step into your highest self through truth, grace, and the unique design of your "wellness circle." A real energetic connection of who you are, binding the three lines of wellness: mind, body, and soul. In an ever-evolving harmony of greatness, rooted in reinvention, you'll define your lines of wellness through self-discovery, exposing the invisible glue partnered to bind the lines together—a call for a connection.

Connection Commitment

Come as boldly as you come into truth. Say to yourself, "I am ready; I am able, I am willing." A self-intention, to be raw and real. Find grace in the grind of your truth by surrendering comparison, anxiety, fear, and control. Lean into the reveal by opening your heart through this "connection commitment" to yourself.

Gently place your right hand on your heart or unite your palms at heart center in prayer as you speak goodness to yourself.

"Today, I embrace reinvention through the reveal. I accept what brought me to where I am. I stand rooted in the place that I'm going, and I choose grace in the grind. To find a balance between control and surrender worldly strongholds. I now free my

heart from the disconnection created, by comparison, anxiety, and fear. In my discovery, I'll take what I need from the people, places, and things and release what no longer serves me. I build a foundation of freedom connecting the lines of wellness into my ever-evolving "wellness circle," of mind, body, and soul. In the truth, power, and grace of my authentic self, I humbly accept the unknown, and step into the beauty of knowing the essence of who I am."

The Discovery

"Looking back is a way to sharpen the focus on the things you want to change in your life. I think there's something in the nostalgia that puts a fine point on the here-and-now, and that can be incredibly fascinating and interesting and engaging for the mind." —Sarah Paulson

There is tremendous power in discovery. The courage to sit within yourself to see where you are and set your gaze on where you're going. You take a roll call of awareness to study how each line of wellness plays a part in your journey. Within that observation, you can connect your past with your present to purposefully declare reinvention by revealing sources of weakness, disconnect, or imbalance. Perhaps it's the absence of the connective adhesive, the glue, that solidifies your circle. Together let's discover the truth.

A Beautiful Mind

"The biggest wall you have to climb is the one you build in your mind: Never let your mind talk you out of your dreams, trick you into giving up. Never let your mind become the greatest obstacle to success. To get your mind on the right track, the rest will follow." —Roy T. Bennett, The Light in the Heart

"I was given your name by a friend." The voice on the phone was shaky with hope. "I heard you have a background in mental health, and you utilize that experience in your engagement with your clients. My 12-year-old daughter is in recovery from a rare form of obsessive-compulsive disorder (OCD), called Scrupulosity." (An excessive and debilitating focus on moral or religious fears which holds one captive in a catatonic presence, often rendering them speechless.) "She was encouraged by her therapist to add a physical component to her treatment. My friend felt you might be a good fit for her." A divine connection, orchestrated by God, Aubrey entered my heart. To tap into who she was, and hoped to be again, I needed to capture the essence of her internal and external being—the discovery. Before the onset of illness, Aubrey carried an incredible zest for life. Surrounded by good friends and family, she expressed a beautiful mind of creativity, an active lifestyle through lacrosse, and solidified by faith. A wellness circle was formed.

The signs of OCD arrived in different forms and at different times, all with the common denominator pointing to religious fixation. A mind trap controlled by anxious obsessions, a voice silenced by fear and a body paralyzed by the exhaustion of the fight, Aubrey became a prisoner. With countless misdiagnoses, failed treatments, and unanswered questions, she and her family never gave up hope. It was within the treacherous climb of intensive therapy, the will to get better, and her trust in God, Aubrey began to recover.

She met with me twice a week for personal training and social skill building to develop internal and external confidence. Uncomfortable in her skin and a voice barely heard, we maneuvered with grace. It's when you come to the end of yourself that you learn grace begins. The grace is in the grind. Gifted with divine assistance, we worked through awkward high-fives, conversational homework given by her therapist, and physical strength once weakened and held prisoner by her mind. Slowly, reinvention surfaced as the corners of her mouth turned up, and a light reappeared in her face. The high-fives came without hesitation, turned into hugs, and the voice barely heard began to rise in confidence. A beautiful mind reinvented.

Aubrey continues to build her "wellness circle," a circle once shattered and disconnected by tragedy rebuilt with harmony. Her climb continues as lingering remanence of OCD resides within. She discovered her glue—faith. The thing her illness used to trap her mind was the thing she grabbed ahold of to solidify and save her.

"What kept me going in addition to my family and those who supported and loved me was my faith in God. I began to trust, find peace, strength, and hope in Him. I know I would not feel the same joy without God in my life. It's through Him I got better." — Aubrey

The mind is a powerful gift to be used wisely. Your conscious and subconscious process thoughts, reason with feelings and navigate worldly experiences. We may choose to see a positive past and the shortcomings that contribute to a soul-crushing battle on our well-being. Battle of light vs. darkness represented by comparison, anxiety, control, and fear lead to an internal tug of war of expectation. Judgment and doubt create a vicious cycle of negativity and immense gravitational pull, a beautifully broken line, separating with intent to control and prevent cohesive harmony—your harmony of greatness. You have the final say in how much power negativity has over the mind line of wellness.

As I look back, I'm overcome with emotion by the indomitable will Aubrey had to overpower her mind. A mind of invisible prisons controlling the body and soul. The 17-year-old woman stands today in greatness and decides every day to keep fighting. Aubrey said to me once, "I imagined my future where I was better, doing the things I'm called to do, going to college, getting a job, marrying, and having kids. I believed I would get better. I encourage others to keep fighting, trust in God, and know they can lean on Him. He will give you what you need. He loves you."

Step One: Reveal

The Reinvention Of Your Wellness Circle:

Sit with yourself for a moment and ask, "Is my mind line of wellness powerfully pulling me out of harmony? If so, through discovery, reveal it. Own the things that imprison you. Maybe it's depression, control issues, lack of self-worth. Write down and reflect on your mind's battle of light and dark—self-discovery.

Temporary Home

"For I am fearfully and wonderfully made; marvelous are Your works, and that my soul knows very well." (Psalm 139:14)

God can blow the whistle on you abruptly or sneak up from behind to save you from the unseen, preventing the ultimate destruction. For me, He was a sneaky little bugger. Forever present in my life, God wanted all of me. Not only sometimes or when I found it convenient, which was the type of relationship we had most days. Aware my career consumed all of me; He executed the perfect rescue.

My career focused on physicality. An industry full of judgment and expectation, I was unknowingly becoming unglued.

Mastered by inspiring others, busyness, and attempts to live up to the epitome of health, work began to take a toll on all three lines of my "wellness circle." Self-inflicted stress to exude wellness, be strong in presence and be fully put together weakened my mind and soul, amplifying anxiety. I convinced myself the perceived scrutiny from everyone else was the main root of my burden. Daily living carried on as I hid behind influencing others and building the business—my grind. I practiced what I preached: maintaining a healthy diet, regular exercise, and focused mindfulness. A body representing wholeness, my wellness circle appeared stable, but something was missing—my glue.

Your body is divinely crafted to carry your mind-soul life force into action, gifted to you by God to preserve and honor. An external line of wellness, your body, is significantly impacted and scrutinized by a culture of comparison and worldly pressures. Those pressures feed the darkness of lies which sit in your mind and attack your soul. Insecurity opens the door to a warped sense of being, inviting unseen internal attacks. Superficially strong, the body line of wellness governs your truth, the real you. Keep in mind; surface well-being camouflages the relentless battle of mind and soul.

I've found that the power of living authentically, as God's creation, was sacrificed by a desire to look, feel, and be perfect. Physicality is temporary, shifting urgency in your assignment to proportion the inside with the outside. Work on achieving grace in the grind of the two. Reinvention rendered.

Step Two: Grace in the Grind

Check yourself to get real—raw. Are you hiding behind or hyper-focused on the body line of wellness? If so, investigate. Open your heart to how this affects how you're living. Are you living well or in the complacency of the day to day routines? Allow yourself to work toward your grace in the grind. Write down and reflect on how this line determines the harmony of your wellness circle. Reinvention awaits.

It's A Soul Thang

"What will it profit a man if he gains the whole world and loses his soul?" (Mark 8:36)

A storm was brewing. Enduring years of my grind, I threw myself into work and had slipped into a world of complacency: tired, anxious, and overwhelmed. Was this all I was supposed to become? I reached for a readily welcome partner, a friend with no expectations—wine. Unwind from work: wine. Riddled with worry: wine. Conversational accessory: wine. I thrived in social settings and managed my behavior through moderation. I felt lost.

I sat in the car after my doctor's appointment, tears stinging my cheeks, holding a diagnosis of Hereditary Spastic Paraplegia (a neurological disorder of muscle weakness, decreased balance, and degrees of spasticity in the legs). I questioned God, "What will I become? My body is who I am, and what I do." Witnessing the havoc this illness inflicted upon my grandmother and father sent currents of fear pulsing within. Would I fall victim to an inability to walk and unanticipated falls? My faith reaffirmed my body doesn't define who I am. Physicality is temporary.

I found grace in the grind of an incurable condition. In the perceived loss of myself, He revealed a whole new way of living requiring complete surrender returning to the forever constant in my life, God. Who I am is in Him. My reinvention. My glue. Clarity to live well, determined by God, I began a holistic refinement of my wellness circle. Natural supplementation, an anti-inflammatory diet free of alcohol, mindful movement, and soul searching through my Savior. Me redefined and rescued.

Your soul is a divine source, encompassing the essence of your higher self. A light created for you by God to nurture and protect. A powerful embodiment of understanding and wisdom by your moral and emotional nature, trademarked with your identity to live abundantly. Your soul, the keeper of your heart, has emotions of fear and love that store the knowledge of life's circumstances. The soul line is divinely powerful yet influenced by your thoughts, external forces, and the paralyzing lies that hold captive the light abundantly given to you. It makes decisions, the good and the bad. These values bestowed upon you measured by eternal quality, the severity of loss, the allowance of darkness, and the willingness to live by faith. Forever living, your soul, made in the image of God, a most prized possession. There is a line of wellness gifted to you.

Step Three: Soul Search

Sit quietly in your space. Ask yourself, "Who am I? What is my trademark?" Listen to what calls your soul line of wellness to surrender. "Do I need to be rescued?" In surrender, the truth from your reveal sets the reinvention of your wellness circle into action. Who or what will you call?

Your Wellness Circle

"Be strong and courageous. Do not be afraid or terrified because of them, for the Lord your God goes with you; he will never leave you nor forsake you." (Deuteronomy 31:6)

Living well takes work, and a willingness to surrender. "I am ready; I am able, I am willing." There is a call to connect the three lines of wellness; mind, body, and soul—an ever-evolving harmonic circle of greatness. My hope is for you to get raw and real, discover the grace in the grind, and lean into the reveal. Rise from life's challenges. Solidify your circle with the glue that binds, armoring against comparison, anxiety, fear, and control. You get to decide.

Today, be in prayer and petition. Ask God to lead you through this time of self-discovery to open your heart to reinvention. Remember, you are chosen, and you are worthy of living well!

"For we are God's masterpiece. He has created us anew in Christ Jesus so we can do the good things planned for us long ago." (Ephesians 2:10)

CHAPTER

Seventeen

Shape Your Greatness Through Inquiry, Intuition And Trust
By Nikki Pollard

NIKKI POLLARD

Nikki Pollard is a certified nutritional consultant, business coach, and entrepreneur. Her mission is to help others step into their power for physical, mental, spiritual and financial wellness. She's a wife, mother and Christ-follower. She taught high school English before deciding to work from home, through commercial acting. She loves her church and enjoys making their video announcements. Professionally, her true calling is to empower and inspire others. A health crisis brought a new passion for understanding the role nutrition plays on quality of life. In May 2013, she aligned herself with Isagenix, a holistic health and wellness company. It started with the health of her family and inner circle. It quickly evolved into passive income, and then it blossomed into a lucrative network marketing business enriching thousands of lives. She continues to grow and learn while partnering with like-minded, inspiring world-changers.

nepollard@yahoo.com

grasptruewellness.isagenix.com

Acknowledgments

I appreciate my family and friends and their constant encouragement and support. Greg, my husband, thanks for your belief in me throughout life's twists and turns. You demonstrate for us strength, dedication and hard work. Thanks to my parents who've modeled unconditional love and good communication. I'm grateful for my kids, Nathan and Maddie, who remind me to slow down, laugh and love often, and not take life too seriously. Thanks Patti Ann Ridgway for being a mentor and friend who reminds me to lean into God, trusting Him no matter what. Thanks to my dear friend, Laura Rudacille, for inviting me to collaborate on this project along with Kyra Schaefer, both ladies whose talent and hearts I admire. I'm grateful for each person I've had the honor to work with over the years, and I value each relationship, friendship, and partnership to come.

Shape Your Greatness Through Inquiry, Intuition And Trust
By Nikki Pollard

O ur stories unfold. We can watch reactively or stand empowered, trusting the outcome, allowing the mold that holds us to give a little, as it shapes us into better versions of ourselves. This idea of a new "us" feels uncomfortable, distant, and foreign, like stepping into a new class, trying new foods, or driving our first car. Without growth, we become stagnant and stuck. We innately desire more than "a state of merely existing." Some decide and take action on their own, while others fall into it through an unwelcome force.

In 2010, we were blind-sided. My seemingly, healthy 36-year old husband was in severe heart failure, "a walking time-bomb," they called him. I'd stepped away from my nine-year teaching career to be at home with the kids, ages one and three, and fear and uncertainty consumed me. I needed to stay positive, smile, and carry the family, so I held those feelings close. The weight was heavy, and I found solace in those rare, alone times of mowing the yard when the sound of the mower would drown out my prayers and screams to God.

We followed instructions precisely, floundering through grocery stores, reading sodium levels on labels and menus, and taking the numerous medications, optimistic for our three-month follow-up. Our optimism was dashed, learning his heart was still functioning at merely 10 percent. Restored hope came in the form of a pacemaker/defibrillator implanted in his chest. Doctors had no words when this failed to help, and we found ourselves visiting a transplant team.

Desperately, we looked beyond ourselves for answers, strengthened, incessant prayer guiding us. The bigger question no doctor asked was, "Why was he sick?" He was young, looked healthy, and had recently planted 18 trees in our backyard. He went to the gym and ate okay. Little by little, I educated myself, sorted through layers of information, and began to make changes in our family. Awareness and shifts weren't easy. I clung to what needed to be addressed internally: nutrient deficiencies, toxicity, and inflammation.

Sickness doesn't suddenly "get" us. Our state is determined by how we live and love, how we deal with stress, what we eat and drink, and how well we sleep. Our cells and our organs were designed beautifully, and they miraculously give us warning signs long before disaster hits. We've become adept at ignoring and masking symptoms we should be embracing. Headaches can stem from dehydration, stress, a nutrient deficiency or food sensitivity, hormonal imbalances or muscle tension. We're taught to pop a pill, without giving it a second thought. Slowing down, investigating the root issue and asking "Why?" is something we don't do. For lasting change or resolution, it's important to get curious and dig deep. Whether living a healthier lifestyle or healing relationships, overcoming limiting beliefs or stepping into your dreams, transformation requires mindset work.

When challenges come, we similarly want easy and quick resolutions, instructions and steps to "do." Instead, it's important to step into the process intuitively, taking a broader vantage point where we become self-reflective, actively listening and feeling our way through the entire journey, embracing the "highs," expecting the "lows," and asking the scary questions along the way. These questions can rip us right open, painfully exposing what's easier not to deal with: past failures, hurts, injustices, anger, insecurities, or fear.

Empowerment comes with a heavy yet liberating burden. Feeling the emotions and taking steps to work through them is arduous. When I finally asked why Greg was sick, life became harder than passively taking a pill. Digging and learning brought deeper layers of questions. I learned there isn't any single answer or definitive endpoint when we can finally say, "Okay. That's it. I'm there and I get it." Turning over one stone at a time feels like going in circles, yet we need to keep moving our feet and focusing on what's important to us.

I'll never forget driving the kids home from the soccer field, biting my nails as I awaited Greg's phone call. Another follow-up echocardiogram brought the usual pit in my stomach.

"Where are you? Can you pull over?" I braced myself and parked the car. "My heart is back to normal. The doctors can't explain it." The tears still come when I think back to this moment of shock, disbelief, gratitude and overwhelm.

What we can't see is the tapestry being woven along this ugly yet beautiful journey of self-discovery. We never know the lives we're touching and inspiring as we fumble through it. Certainly, the forces outside ourselves constantly work on our behalf: divinely inspired encounters, little magic moments, or words of encouragement at precisely the perfect time. Our newfound knowledge was a piece of the puzzle, while thousands of prayers gave us hope.

God masterfully orchestrated the miraculous healing no doctor could explain. He didn't stop there, though, since the journey continues beyond us. God connected me to a bigger vision, company and vehicle bringing a slice of hope and wellness to thousands of others. I'm beginning to see and appreciate this ripple effect we have on one another. My husband was sick. I was angry. That could have been the end of the story, but it wasn't. I listened to my heart and God's voice and took action. I know it's not rainbows and butterflies from here on out. Tougher times inevitably will come. We will lean into faith, trust, growth and community.

I hope to inspire you to feel overcome with gratitude at who you are and the struggles you've overcome. Greatness and purpose lie within you, far beyond what you see and feel at this moment. One day, you will look back and see your own ripple effect and impact. Where are you now? What frustrates you? In what areas do you seek growth or change? Now, grab your notebook and a pen. Let's get to work digging deep and empowering you to shift the trajectory of your life.

Action Steps

Step One: Decide

Decide to embrace the process with your whole heart. Write it down as a commitment. Make a decision to take action, knowing it will be hard but worth it. Expect challenges. This is your resistance, the only way to build any "muscle." With this mindset, you'll start to welcome challenges, knowing deeper growth and true transformation are coming.

Step Two: Get Real and Raw

1. Your Why:

    Find your "Why" by journaling around these questions. Know that your "why" will probably evolve and change over time, as you grow. What do you want that you don't have? (Health, better relationships, a job that fulfills you, financial security, forgiveness, peace of mind.)

2. Deeper Why:

Once you've written what you want, ponder and write about why you want it. Write it down in as much detail as you can. A meaningful why will enable you to keep going when things get tough.

Example: "I want to lose weight" means nothing.

"I want to lose weight, so I can be around for my grandkids, because I love spending time with them, and I want to see them graduate and get married."

Example: "I want financial security" means nothing.

"I want greater cash flow and less stress each month. I want to be present with the kids and not miss all those 'firsts,' too busy working all the time to make ends meet. I want to free myself and then others. I want a means to help other single mothers struggling."

3. Attaching Emotion:

Think about a poignant, lasting memory from your past, and you automatically feel how you felt at that moment. When I taught literature, we went beyond reading the words of a book. We stepped into the book, trying to feel what the characters felt, and that was lasting, impressionable and relatable, taking our learning to a whole new level.

We want to take your goals to the next level and attach feelings to them, so they're forever imprinted in your mind, heart, and soul. Again, when you hear the negative voices or face the challenges (and you will), you will be able to step back into these feelings as a tool.

Next, reflect and then journal, as if you've achieved that goal. You have overcome what was holding you back! How does this feel? Picture it in detail. Feel it in your heart. Let it settle in. How does it change things for you and those around you? How is life different and richer? Take time to grasp this for it to be effective.

Now, this should be uncomfortable. Take time to imagine things going on the way they are now for you, without any change: six months, one year, 20 years from now. You took no action, and all is the same. How does this feel and look? Be honest with yourself, get raw, and journal.

Good job! You have taken a huge step in getting real with where you are now, how it feels, where you want to go, and how awesome that will feel. Again, you should periodically revisit this exercise as you move along your journey, through victories and setbacks and your personal evolution.

Step 3: Support and Community

As you stay focused on the end-goal, it'll feel abstract and distant. Old patterns and beliefs are deeply rooted, a constant battle within and a natural part of the process. I've found the best way to break through these struggles is to find people who have, or are working to attain, what you want. You need a support team, an inner circle, a tribe! I've coached people in finding health, losing weight, or building wealth, and often they're surrounded by the negativity of friends or family on a different trajectory. Their personal set of limiting beliefs can sabotage unless we have the support system in place and a strong "why" to go with it.

Think about the 5-10 people with whom you spend the most time. Write down those names. Now circle the ones who'll support you or maybe even walk alongside you as part of your team. Who might bring you down? Put a heart around those names and love them where they are in their journey. I'm sure they are working through issues, but it's up to you how you decide to react and how much power you give them.

Next, find your tribe! If you don't have five people circled in your journal, get to work. Who around you has what you want? Join some groups, smaller circles, where you can plug into that positive vibe. We have a private coaching group for health and a separate group for business, where we lean on one another. Maybe for you, it's a networking group, a gym, a church group, or a "survivor" group of whatever obstacle you're overcoming. If you feel you're on the "other" side of hardship, be the light for others, and lead a group! There's no better way to stay in hope and positivity than to help and support others.

Until you achieve your own hope and belief, plugging into positivity and your tribe is vital. Keep building your support team. Communicate and share your successes and struggles. Ask your questions and share your thoughts. As you grow in confidence, begin answering questions and concerns for others, fostering a ripple effect within the community.

Step 4: Doable, Measurable Action Steps

You can have a big "why," a strong support system, and active engagement in a rich community, but you won't shift until you have a plan. It's time to create a master schedule and action steps to move those feet.

People might say they want to lose 100 pounds, learn to speak Spanish or double their income. These goals are attainable for those who commit, once broken down into doable, measurable, baby-action steps.

Schedule Time:

First, assess your reality by taking an honest inventory of what you're willing to change and how much time you can honestly devote. We must be sure our goal and timeframe align. I've coached two neighbors, who shared a goal of releasing 30 pounds. Theresa, determined to take an aggressive approach, stuck 100% to the system and surpassed her goal by three months, doubling it in a few more months. Jaimee, who had failed so many other "diets," wanted to take a more moderate approach, allowing herself more leeway here and there. Both succeeded by personalizing their realistic and doable approach, losing and now maintaining for several years.

Similarly, if your goal is to increase your income or learn a new language, how much time are you willing to devote to action? If you have three hours per week to allot to your goal, you can achieve it, but perhaps not as quickly as someone who has 15 hours per week.

Determine Measurable Action Steps:

Figure out a few actions that will move you towards your end-goal. If you've carried a history of failure, start small, and stop comparing yourself to others. Don't set a goal to lose three pounds this week, find three new clients, or pass your first Spanish test, since those are outcomes/achievements we can't directly control. Instead, choose steps you know you can do, that are measurable and will move you in the right direction, while building confidence in success.

Example: I'll follow my wellness plan 90% each day, 10% grace, exercise three times per week, and plug in daily to our Facebook page.

Example: I'll attend a networking event weekly, spend 30 minutes a day following up with potential clients, schedule two one-on-one appointments per week.

Example: I'll take a weekly Spanish class online, study three hours on my own each week, and write weekly to my Spanish pen-pal.

Journal time:

How much time do you have to devote to your "evolution"?

When exactly will this occur each week?

What action will you take each week?

Jot it down, grab your planner or calendar, and schedule it! We schedule appointments with our doctors and dentists, so we need to schedule the time to work towards a better "us." Now, go do it and stay encouraged!

Step 5: Reflect / Celebrate / Adjust

Congratulations! You're in action, working step by step towards your goals. Pace doesn't matter, as long as you're moving. Choose a day to schedule and journal weekly reflections. What are three things you can celebrate? Write them down and take time to feel success, no matter how small it seems. This is key to staying motivated and positive. Where did you fall short, and why? Take time to write down what could be improved and ask questions. Were your action steps doable, or do they need to be adjusted? If they were doable, what got in the way, and how can you adjust next week? Ask for help and keep moving.

We took a dive into empowerment by identifying our "why" and getting in touch with our emotions around it. We've identified our support team and recognized the importance of leaning into the community through the highs and lows. Finally, we scheduled both action steps that are measurable and doable, as well as time to reflect and adjust as we go. This basic flow will get you to your goals. Just hold onto your belief and practice consistency. You've got this!

CHAPTER

Eighteen

The Virtues To
Relationship Freedom
By Rayann Chi

RAYANN CHI

RayAnn Chi has been married to her wonderful husband for almost 20 years. They have three beautiful children together. RayAnn started her career passionately serving others as a hairstylist and makeup artist for 15 years. While enjoying being a stylist, she began to find a passion for fitness and nutrition. She later started an online business as a health and wellness coach. While things were growing rapidly in her business, her marriage began to break down slowly. This was a blessing in disguise, a disruption where it led her to radical self-growth. She became passionately involved in shadow work, working with the subconscious mind and the healing arts. She immersed herself endlessly through research and intensives to later acquiring her professional certificates. As she saw the profound shift and healing in her marriage, and most importantly herself, this made her realize that through this work, she wanted to focus on relationships, shadow work, and subconscious reprogramming. Integrating and embodying this work, RayAnn is a certified Quantum Master Healer, Relationship Coach, and Sacred Sex Educator.

You can find her at www.shadowworkalchemy.com
IG: shadowworkalchemy
FB page: shadowworkalchemy

Acknowledgments

First of, all the praise and gratitude goes to none other than the pure loving energy of God. I will not be able to do anything without this magnificent source. Within me and by my side, my true refuge. Allowing me to have these beautiful souls in my life...Much appreciation to my loving and most thoughtful husband Johnny who has been my ride or die, my soulmate. My pillar of strength and has always supported me through my dreams, goals, and aspirations. Thank you for seeing it through with me. I am so lucky to have you! To the most amazing children that ever existed in my world! Tiwa, Kaya, and Luna. You all are always so patient with me. Understanding and pushing me through when some days can feel cloudy. To my one and only sister Ruth Ann who is always there when I need her. Thank you for always inspiring me and being my cheerleader. Thank you to my family and friends that I did not mention. Lastly, to my dearest Facebook friends, you know who you are! I am so thankful that we crossed paths. I love you all!

The Virtues To Relationship Freedom
By Rayann Chi

The Virtues of Relationship Freedom

I will cover the two virtues which I find the most helpful: *Honor and Grace*. You will learn how seven virtues not only saved my marriage, but also allowed my husband and I to have freedom.

When I say freedom, this is not the kind of freedom where one does whatever he or she wants. It's where there is deliverance, liberation, and release. These virtues came to me when my husband and I were on the brink of separation and possible divorce. In the midst of chaos, I had to ask myself what I did wrong. There are three sides to every story: my side, his side, and the truth. By now, I learned that the only way I could move forward was to take responsibility for my actions and ask myself what it is that I've done, and how I could make things better.

I wanted a solution that could be easily implemented not only in my daily life, but in my husband's as well. For days, I reflected and meditated on this question, until one day, it finally came. An inspired action led me to quickly act on it as it persisted in my mind. When these types of inspired actions arrive, you need to act fast; otherwise it may never come back. I know these always come for a reason, so I wrote them down.

One by one, I researched and studied each virtue to have an in-depth understanding of them. As I started to implement the virtues in my marriage, I began to see tremendous growth. I began to work on deep-seated subconscious blocks that I realized during my chaos. This was a blessing in disguise. I became more conscious of understanding why my marriage was the way it was. It brought on profound healing and allowed me to go deeper into what seemed to be an uncomfortable abyss. There were many blocks my husband and I had to break through. We both became aware that what seemed to be a never-ending cycle were manifestations of an old paradigm. A paradigm we have adapted to since the young age of 18.

Together we persisted and had the tenacity to thrive in our marriage. We divorced our old marriage and started to create a new one based on our new beliefs. Breakthroughs were happening which I had only dreamed of and cycles finally came to an end. This not only liberated me, but my husband as well. It was a form of a long overdue release. *It was freedom.*

"Reacting, in the same way, keeps you bound to the lesson and you get in this karmic loop. When you are presented with the same situations over and over, you have to do something different. The karmic cycle ends when you decide to no longer participate; break the chains."—Sadhguru

When you finally understand the lesson and know that change must be done for your relationship to improve, you do it. Because it is no longer an option, it is mandatory.

Sometimes the hardest thing to do is to surrender. You want to have control over yourself and your partner. You try so hard to plan and prevent things from happening. You control things because of fear of what will happen if you don't. Surrender means to stop fighting. Stop fighting with yourself and with your partner. Stop fighting with God and the natural flow of things. In a relationship, you must choose your battles, and that also means choosing to surrender when it is most necessary. We resist letting go when needed because we fear what would happen if we allowed ourselves to be vulnerable, to let down our walls, or to give up control completely. The art of surrender is the process of growth. It takes a lot of emotional and mental maturity to let go. Allow yourself to lean into the phrase *let go and let God.*

Honor

To have honor in your relationship means holding your partner in high regard. It's having high respect for them and it is esteem at the highest level. Honor is the feeling of pride and pleasure resulting when respect is shown. When someone honors you, they recognize and see your value and worth. Honor is a gift you should give yourself, and you shouldn't have to worry about obtaining it. To honor is also fulfilling an agreement you made with your partner.

This agreement refers to the vows you made before you decided to commit to one another. When you remember to honor your partner, it reminds you to appreciate them. When you appreciate something and regard it highly, the likelihood of you mistreating it would be minimal. Let's take a high-end purchase you made or something that cost a significant amount of money. Do you treat it carelessly? Hopefully, your answer is "No." It's easy to get caught up with your circumstances, and easy to forget why you committed in the first place. When you remind yourself that the person with whom you made a vow is more valuable than your high-end purchase, you won't be so quick to forget to honor them. Honoring your partner is also remembering to honor yourself. Honor is a core value because when you know your worth and your value, honor is automatic.

Knowing your self-worth and having healthy self-esteem is an integral practice of honoring yourself. If you are someone who may have low esteem, then it's important to know what this looks like. Although I am talking about relationships, the most important one is with yourself. It is amazing how highly dependent a person can be on other people when they haven't learned how to depend on themselves. This means depending on oneself for their happiness and not having the need to find validation from others constantly. When a breakup happens, it is natural to be saddened by the feelings and thoughts of losing that person in the relationship. Losing yourself in a relationship is like death. To have high self-esteem is to have confidence in your worth or abilities and know you are worthy of happiness. It is also self-efficacy.

Self-efficacy is basically your ability to think for yourself and direct your life. Answer these questions and rank yourself on a scale from 1-10:

How competent do you feel that you can create a good life for yourself?

How competent do you feel that you can take care of yourself and handle things accordingly?

Scoring a four and below to those questions could mean you have low efficacy. 5-7 is mid-range, and 8-10 is high self-efficacy.

Another part of self-esteem is self-respect:

How much do you respect yourself?

Do you believe you have the right to be happy?

Do you believe that people in your relationships must treat you well and that you deserve it?

If you scored a four or less, your level self-respect needs some attention. You may be devaluing your happiness, and you potentially have felt like a doormat. People find it easy to victimize others with low self-respect.

Self-esteem has everything to do with your mindset and who you think you are: your beliefs and your self-image. It is your inner game, your psychology at play. The most honest thing you can do is to recognize if you have healthy self-esteem or not. If you rank yourself a four and below, then you need to acknowledge it and tell yourself that you have a low self-esteem issue, it's not the end of the world and that you are not to blame.

It's important not to get discouraged. This is you being honest with yourself. This is an honest evaluation of where you are right now, and you recognize that you have work to do. You are going to want to fix this problem, so the first step in fixing a problem is to recognize that you have one. Remember that self-esteem can fluctuate or change during your lifetime. If you once had developed healthy self-esteem, you could have dimmed yourself so that others wouldn't notice you.

The good news is that most of this can be sorted out. The program you are operating on can be reprogrammed. You can always reach out for help to get you back to a healthy level of self-esteem. This, in turn, will make dramatic improvements in your relationships. Change always starts with you. When you change, naturally the people around will. Ultimately, you are responsible for what you allow into your life.

"The tragedy of many people's lives is that they look for self-esteem in every direction except within...and so they fail in their search." —Nathaniel Branden

To strengthen and grow your relationship, it's important first to know and evaluate how it is doing. You need to be willing, to be honest, and accept without denial or evasion. An attitude of acceptance is choosing to value your partner and treat your partner with respect. This goes two ways. As you choose to act on acceptance, you must also be honest with yourself and have self-acceptance. This means that you are choosing to value yourself, treat yourself with respect and stand up for your right to be in the relationship. You also must have the willingness to want to experience your partner *as is*. They are who they are, feel what they feel, and think what they think. We shouldn't disown the facts presented to us of who they are being at a particular moment.

Grace

This leads us to the virtue of grace. Grace is what you receive when you have messed up, fallen down, and made wrong choices. Grace does not focus on failed expectations and the shortcomings of your partner. Sometimes the expectations you place on your partner are higher than they can attain. In theology, the meaning of grace is an essential way which God expresses love for us. The Oxford dictionary defines grace as the free and unmerited favor of God.

I am using God as an example by means of grace because God perfectly and consistently exemplifies grace because *It* is by nature gracious. We often struggle to extend grace. This can be true in a relationship. How can you tell if grace is lacking in your relationship with your partner?

Consider the following questions and answer them as truthfully and as quickly as possible:

1. Does your partner have certain behaviors or quirks that irritate you?
2. Are you trying to change your partner to no avail?

3. Do you expect your partner to read your mind, decode your body language or meet all your needs perfectly, every single time?
4. Do you constantly micromanage and try to control your partner's every move?
5. Do you assume the worst about your partner without giving them the benefit of the doubt and jumping to negative conclusions?
6. Do you find yourself regularly losing patience and getting snippy with your partner?
7. Are you overcritical and tend to nitpick?

If you answered "Yes" to the questions, then perhaps you may be going through a difficult season in your relationship. It's possible that grace has been replaced by deep-seated hurt, frustration, and resentment. These painful feelings toward your partner could have been slowly building up, and in turn, have made you shut down or harden.

Don't fret! There is hope.

Grace is a virtue similar to tolerance. Tolerance is the ability or willingness to endure the existence of opinions or behaviors that one does not necessarily agree with. It's also the capacity to endure continued subjection to something. I am not saying that you should be a doormat and have tolerance for everything. To tolerate things in a relationship is to be able to choose your battles.

Would you waste your precious time and energy being upset with your partner if he or she forgot to put away the dishes the night before, knowing it was his or her turn? Would you be upset if he or she came home with the wrong item from the grocery store, especially if you specifically asked for it? These are small examples, but you get my point. In a relationship, battles have to be chosen, in which this case, we compromise and have tolerance for the rest.

Grace has a way of recalibrating your relationship. So how can you emulate God and apply this amazing gift within your relationship? *You practice it.*

Practicing grace is exactly what you need from your partner and vice versa. It's a commitment to love each other exactly where you both are. Like acceptance, grace looks past the things your partner does that frustrates you so that you can see what's true about him or her.

It's about remembering who your partner is on the inside, not how they are irritating you at the moment. True love isn't about loving one hundred different people; it's about loving the one hundred different versions of the same person you decided to commit to. Grace believes the best about your partner. It moves both of you forward through the messiness of a particular situation or behavior.

"Everyone makes mistakes in life, but that doesn't mean they have to pay for them for the rest of their life. Sometimes good people make bad choices. It doesn't mean they're bad; it means they're human." —Unknown

Grace gives the benefit of the doubt, a powerful attribute to this virtue. Instead of making assumptions about your partner's motives, grace tries to understand where he or she is coming from. It forces you to ask, "I know your heart even though your present actions are perplexing. Help me understand what is going on."

Ultimately, it will take two people to make a relationship work, and one way to improve things is to interject grace. When both parties are grace-giving to each other, the relationship can soar.

In conclusion, be kind, tenderhearted, and forgiving of one another. Give your partner grace freely as God does. After all, as you grow and expand together in your relationship, along comes trials and struggles. We all have skeletons in our closets, and we are bound to make mistakes. Don't let that be the reason you give up on your partner. Be grateful and learn to move your relationship forward with grace.

CHAPTER

Nineteen

Winning Is A Habit
By Rich Orndoff

RICH ORNDOFF

Rich Orndoff is a life coach, clinical hypnotherapist, NLP and EFT practitioner in Phoenix, Arizona. Rich's passion is assisting people in healing and transforming their lives. He began his coaching career at the age of 15, teaching martial arts and holds advanced rankings in five martial arts which he continues to both study and teach. A self-described psychology and neuroscience geek, he continues to pursue his passion for healing modalities. He grew up in the wilds of the Arizona desert and believes that regular connection to nature is important for mental health. Rich's hobbies of adventure, racing, orienteering, hiking, mountain biking, and backpacking incorporate his love of intense activity and the outdoors. He can be reached for sessions, both online and in person, through his private practice, Invictus Life. Visit his website at www.fulcrumcoaching.net for booking sessions, catching up with his blog, inquiries, and interesting content.

Acknowledgments

So much of who and what I am today is a direct gift from many others, for more people than I can effectively list here. Dr. Amy Rosner, my coach, hypnotherapist, professional mentor, and friend; you have positively affected my life in ways beyond measure. Master Peter Hill, you have been an influence throughout my entire adult life, and I still regularly quote our conversations and reference all the books you strongly encouraged me to read. To my amazing tribe of warrior souls who accept me for who I am and allow me to experiment on their brains each time I'm ready to roll out a new technique; you are all amazing human beings and I am privileged to know you all. Many thanks to all of you, and the instructors, coaches, and managers from whom I have learned so much.

Winning Is A Habit
By Rich Orndoff

The Foundation of Lasting Success: Proven Principles

If you're reading this book, it is because you wish to improve the quality of your experience on this planet. However, only by incorporating a handful of core concepts will you be able to maximize its wisdom and prevent it from becoming another interesting read occupying space on the bookshelf.

Realize that the success of anything we do in life, in any arena, is predicated on understanding and mastering the fundamental skills of that activity. In fact, these primary principles are so critical, it is essentially impossible to succeed without them in our foundation.

Imagine trying to build your dream house with a shoddy foundation for its base. It might have elaborate architecture, sturdy walls, marble support columns, and a gorgeous roof; yet it will inevitably crumble to the earth as the foundation cracks.

First Things First: Developing a Winning Mindset

A mindset is a mixture of what we are thinking and feeling, which drives our actions. Developing a winning mindset as our foundation is imperative to achieving anything worthwhile in life. The components of this way of thinking comprise the powerful mental habits that we must develop to achieve any lasting success. Without incorporating these habits, we are too easily distracted, knocked off course, repeatedly detoured, or flat out defeated. Every single thought we have or thing we do is a habit, so it is important to appreciate the immense power of habits to command our lives.

This topic alone could be an entire book with each aspect being its own chapter, and I am expanding on each of these areas in a special section of my blog through my website. However, I am going to share three of the central components to a winning mindset right here:

Action, consistency, and resiliency.

Focusing on these three elements will enhance all other habits and beliefs we are working on mastering and keeping us moving forward in our lives.

Fundamentals Bootcamp

We are often afflicted with the belief that something must be complex to be of high value. We want cutting-edge ideas, the hot hack of the day, the next big thing, and 'outside the box thinking.' Most of the things which will move you forward are already 'inside the box' in the form of ideas, practices, and tools which are well-established and time has proven. Regarding the laws of human dynamics, there ain't nothin' new under the sun!

The only reason we don't see their immense power, and easily overlook them, is that we are not consistently using them. It doesn't get any simpler than that. My goal here is to provide you with simple, powerful, tangible ideas. Each of these will help build the habits which will build the "you" that you most want. Integrating these ideas will determine the success of every other tool or process you attempt.

I practice a high-concept/low-tech approach. Every idea and tool presented here is distilled and simple to implement, while still rich with proven principles. Each section is followed by my top three professional tips for incorporating each component.

The questions I invite you to ask yourself as you move through this chapter are:

How can these core concepts be applied in my life?

What can I gain today from incorporating these into my life?

What will my life look like if I incorporate these powerful ideas?

Action: Ready. Fire! Aim.

It is said that 'knowledge is power.' I'm here to dispute that adage because it is not accurate. Knowledge is *not* power. Knowledge is opportunity. It is the opportunity to improve, to grow, to change, to evolve and to rise above our former lives into something much greater. Thus, knowing is not enough. *Action* is power.

"Whatever you can do or dream you can, begin it. Boldness has genius, power, and magic in it."—Johann Wolfgang von Goethe

To build the habit of taking action, we first need to develop a deep appreciation and connection with the habit of taking action. Action gets things done, moves us forward, and builds the life we want. You already know enough to begin anything you wish or could have the basic steps within minutes. How many strategies, tips, and tools do you already know on any subject versus how many of them are you consistently incorporating? The only way to begin taking action is to do it.

This raises an important subject. If you find that taking action in any area is a challenge for you, it is necessary to find out the cause. What is preventing you from either starting or finishing?

Do you think you are a procrastinator? I have been doing this work for a long while, and I don't believe in procrastination. I have never seen a single case of it. What I do see is resistance, avoidance, self-limiting beliefs, old stories, fears, and ineffective mental habits which prevent people from acting. If we don't uncover the source of these internal limits and obstacles, and resolve them, we will forever be at their mercy.

A popular phrase in self-development is 'do your work,' referring to internal healing and reprogramming. 'Work' is not only a noun but also a verb. If we are going to get past our internal limits, we must take consistent action until the issue is completely resolved. If we are prescribed a ten-day course of antibiotics, we don't stop taking them after six days if we start feeling better. Resolving our fears, traumas, and viral programming can take time and courage. Remain persistent, and you will achieve a fulfilling life of freedom, accomplishment, and purpose. This is the power of taking decisive action.

Pro Tip #1: Focus on what is within your control.

Before rising each morning, ask yourself, "What action can I take today that will move me closer to my goals?" In any given situation, ask yourself, "What is one action I can take right now that will improve this circumstance?" Listen for those answers and act on them.

Pro Tip #2: Recognize you are ready *now*.

You have enough information to act. Doing more research is a form of avoidance, and we risk getting stuck. Remember, a basic plan executed passionately today is better than the perfect plan put into action next week.

Pro Tip #3: Just do it.

The best way to learn to take action is to be intentional. Right now. On anything. Yes, it is that easy.

Consistency: There is Magic in Momentum

Consistency is action applied daily. Do we get more fitness gains from exercising for 90 minutes once a week or 30 minutes five times per week? You wouldn't build a campfire by piling on all your wood into the pit right away, striking the blaze, watching the flames roar like mad until it soon goes out. Yet this is an accurate metaphor for how most of us approach personal development. We get excited, lay out a highly ambitious plan, launch headlong into our project, and then burn out before we get to enjoy the process. Or we run out of wood due to lack of preparation. In anything we do, consistent daily action is the key to success. Consistency builds momentum, confidence, and motivation from regular wins.

Seeing forward progress consistently reinforces our behavior with a reward of healthy, positive feelings. This is the key to building new, powerful habits: repetition of action and positive reward. This is how big progress is made over time, step by step, day by day. There is so much magic in a having a sense of momentum that we should factor it into all our plans.

Focus on appreciating your daily wins to keep moving forward instead of judging yourself on whether you have achieved a goal. By realizing that this is a cause-and-effect-driven universe, we can begin to see that when we practice the right actions, we will inevitably receive the results we desire. Stacking up the small wins is motivating because there are no small wins.

Create a vision of the future which deeply inspires you. Let it pull you forward with passion as you recognize the beauty of the life you can live. Focus on it daily, allow yourself to want it, and let this vision motivate you to act every day.

Pro Tip #1: Harness the power of technology.

Set a reminder, an alarm, or create a task that will pop-up. If you need a recurring reminder to act, it's right in the palm of your hand.

Pro Tip #2: Have a healthy sense of urgency.

"The problem is you think you have time." —Buddha

Life is the ultimate game, and the game clock is always running. There is no overtime; there are no extra innings. Once our time expires, that's it. Do you want to use it, or not? There is no middle ground here.

Pro Tip #3: Practice kaizen: the one-minute principle.

This concept originated in Japan and centers around the powerful practice of building new habits starting with one minute each day, at the same time. Are you struggling to develop the habit of meditating for ten minutes each morning? Try it kaizen-style for the first week. As your brain gains an understanding of what you want, it will become easier to meditate for longer periods. This works for any new habit.

Resiliency: Suck it Up, Buttercup

What keeps us from reading a book or attending a workshop on personal development and forever soaring off into the cosmos? It's called life. Life can happen to us, at times, knocking us off course or completely off our feet. It is going to happen. Not if, but when.

"Getting knocked down in life is a given. Getting up and moving forward is a choice." —Anonymous

Cultivating the critical mental skill of resilience allows us to navigate the storms of life and continue forward on our chosen route despite setbacks. Mental toughness is like any other skill and can be developed through regular practice. Choose to win and commit to overcome any obstacle.

Focus on progress, not perfection. Too often, we see things in life as 'pass-fail' exercises. "I did it right," or "I did it wrong." "I was good at it," or "I was bad at it." "I won," or "I lost." These expressions of black and white thinking block us from seeing where we are succeeding. Adopting this philosophy of 'progress, not perfection' allows us to begin right now, and gives us the freedom to learn, grow, and improve as we go. Notice yourself getting better as you move forward because you certainly will once you start taking action. If you are uncomfortable during this transition, you are doing it right.

The positive effects of physical activity on our mental process is the most overlooked aspect of average personal development programs. You cannot make any significant changes to your mind without also engaging your body. The vast benefits of regular exercise are so well-documented that I won't waste our time recounting them. Regularly challenging your body enhances confidence and build determination, endurance, and raw grit which are all aspects of resilience. Pick your passion: endurance sports, yoga, martial arts, heavy lifting, roller skating. A regular mixture of activities is best and walk every day. Get sweaty. Get dirty. Get tough. Have fun.

Pro Tip #1: Embrace adversity.

Realize that living things are strengthened by struggle. We require challenges to learn and grow. You need not only a struggle but this particular struggle.

Pro Tip #2: Optimism enhances enthusiasm.

It is easier to get through the hard moments when we believe that everything is going to be okay, and everything *is* going to be okay. Once we accept that there is a solution for every problem, we respond to challenges with higher levels of flexibility, creativity, and resourcefulness. Aren't these at the core of problem-solving?

Pro Tip #3: Laugh.

Laughter is priceless in the face of adversity, even when it is forced or unrelated to the issue at hand. We can find a source of humor at any time, even if it is amusement with our reactions. When I hit a wall of adversity, whether physically during a race or when I need to shift my state in a difficult circumstance, I often playfully tease myself with the mantra: "Suck it up, Buttercup." I say this with a smile as a reminder that I can get up, keep going, and find a way forward.

I invite you to make the decision to adopt the concepts outlined above—right here, right now. A decision does not automatically equal implementation. However, it does allow us to begin expanding and opening the doors inside of ourselves for more light to get in.

Final Thought: Know When to Ask for Help

Your desire for a brighter and more fulfilling life has motivated you to purchase this book and take action. This is the real source of your power, because in the end, *you* and you alone are the captain of your fate and the hero of your story.

However, there are circumstances in our lives which we cannot overcome on our own. We all require assistance. There is a primal synergy that happens when human beings hear and assist each other. Reach out for help when you come upon a situation you cannot easily resolve yourself. I held onto my pain for far too long because I did not know it could be resolved. The longer you wait, the longer you live with it, and the more damage it does. Act sooner.

Be kind to yourself, you are a work in progress and human.

I highly value coaching, and it is the core modality in every session I do. Through this process, we naturally uncover the client's self-limiting beliefs in the form of unresolved grief, trauma, or other emotional damage from childhood or tragedy. This is where I bring in additional modalities like hypnotherapy, NLP, EFT, and others to pick up where regular coaching tools leave off. Through these resources, we can release those limiting factors, repair damage and instill the programming of a winning mindset. I have seen beautiful examples of healing take place inside myself and my amazing clients. It is real.

Anything you wish to heal, you can heal.

Anything you wish to overcome, you can overcome.

Anything you wish to achieve, you can achieve.

Anything you wish to become, you will become.

Now go get it, whatever it is for you.

CHAPTER

Twenty

Write From The Heart And Unlock Your Authentic Story
By Shanda Trofe

SHANDA TROFE

Shanda Trofe is an independent publisher and author coach specializing in book-writing and marketing strategies for authors, coaches, healers and entrepreneurs. Her passion lies in helping those who are called to share a message with the world to find their voice and connect to their authentic, heartfelt story. She believes that a life rich with experience makes for a great message, and she enjoys working with authors throughout the entire process, from idea to publication.

As the Founder of *Spiritual Writers Network* and President & CEO of *Transcendent Publishing*, Shanda has been helping authors realize their writing and publishing goals since 2012. She is the bestselling author of several books including *Authorpreneur* and the *2019 Book-Writing Planner*. Learn more:

www.shandatrofe.com; www.facebook.com/shandatrofe

Write From The Heart And Unlock Your Authentic Story By Shanda Trofe

Years ago, when I set out to name my author coaching business, *Write from the Heart* came so clearly to me. At that time, I was being called to create a program for aspiring authors to get their voices heard. But not just aspiring authors, *anyone* with a message to share and a desire to share that message with the world. That was my mission, and I knew in my heart it was, and still is, my life's work.

What began to happen as I started to uncover my true calling is I began to attract people to me who had a deep-seated desire to share their story through the written word, many of whom didn't consider themselves writers, yet they felt compelled to share their experiences in an attempt to help others on a similar journey. After all, our lives are filled with highs and lows, joys and heartaches, gains and losses. At one point or another, we all encounter things that test our strength and enlighten us as we emerge on the other side of adversity.

For many, a life rich with lessons and wisdom seems almost selfish to keep to ourselves, and that's why many of us are called to write, yet this is where the catch-22 comes in for aspiring authors. They have a story inside them, yet they're held back by fear, self-doubt and self-sabotaging thoughts.

These are precisely the type of writers that I typically end up working with, to my delight! So, how do I take someone without any technical training as a writer and move them through the process, from idea to publication? With one simple premise: write from the heart.

When we connect to our heart-center, that's when our finest writing emerges. When we share openly and honestly, and allow ourselves to be vulnerable, we connect our readers to us and to our story. When we can truly open up and share with the intention to serve, heal and inspire our readers with our truth, the message strengthens and touches our readers on a deeper level.

However, I've found there are a few things that typically stop writers from doing this. The ego will almost always try to creep in and stop you in your tracks, so knowing this going into your writing journey will help you recognize the self-sabotaging thoughts as they arise. Almost all writers experience thoughts and feelings of fear and self-doubt along the way, but when you can train yourself to recognize and dismiss these thoughts as they come, you will overcome the roadblocks and obstacles that many writers face. These are the obstacles that stop many would-be authors from completing their manuscripts in the first place.

If you have a desire to share your message with the world, I'm here to tell you, that message was placed inside your heart for a reason. The key is to connect to your heart-center and let the story emerge effortlessly. Here are a few tips to get you started:

1. **Write for yourself first.** The first draft is just you telling yourself the story; getting it from inside you and onto the paper (or the computer) so that you have some content to work with. First-time authors tend to worry: *who will want to read this? Is this any good? Has this all been done before? What will my family think?* Those are the exact thoughts you need to recognize and dismiss as quickly as they show up. Write your first draft as openly

and freely as possible. Let it all out—the good, the bad, the ugly, the *truth.*

"Don't try to figure out what other people want to hear from you; figure out what you have to say. It's the one and only thing you have to offer."– Barbara Kingsolver

2.   **The only way out is through.** Let the emotion bubble to the surface and write through it. If you find that it's too painful to reopen old wounds and relive certain situations, that's a clear indication that you've yet to process those emotions and you've buried them deep inside. The practice of writing itself can be healing and therapeutic, but often that means reliving the experience. Writing a book not only helps the reader; oftentimes it heals the author in the process as well.

3.   **Let it flow.** If you find yourself wondering how much you should share, pretend you are writing in your personal journal and let it flow freely. You will have many more drafts of your book before it is publication-ready. You can always edit out what you don't want to share later, but for now, write it for you and write it all. The more content you have to work with, the easier it will be later to craft your book. We are not worried so much about structure with the first draft; there will be plenty of time for that in future revisions. For now, compile as much content as you can.

"I'm writing a first draft and reminding myself that I'm simply shoveling sand into a box so I can later build castles." ~ Shannon Hale

4. **Schedule your self-editing time separately from your writing time.** There's a time for revision, but not

during your dedicated writing time. When you edit as you write, you are constantly switching back and forth from the creative side of the brain to the analytical side. This interrupts the flow of creativity and each time you stop, it takes approximately 20 minutes of uninterrupted writing to get it back. If you desire to have one of those writing sessions where the words seem to pour out of you, place your hand on your heart, connect to your heart-center, and then begin writing freely without stopping to second-guess word choices. Chances are, you'll look back at your writing later and find you're impressed by what emerged.

If you have a story inside you or a deep calling to share your message with the world, you don't have to be a trained writer to write your book. You can always hire editors or writing/author coaches to help improve upon your writing and strengthen your story. In the meantime, I'd be willing to bet if you sit down with the intention to write from the heart and follow the steps I've laid out for you here, you'll find that you can write better than expected.

Now you're probably wondering how to map out your book-writing journey. If you have a book inside you and you're being guided to write, chances are you've had this idea for some time. Oftentimes not knowing where or *how* to get started is the only thing holding us back from sharing our message with the world. Spending some time developing your book idea may prove to be the most beneficial point in the book-writing process, and yet it's often the same place where writers get stuck and abandon the project in frustration. I am going to make this process seamless for you, so you'll start with an idea in mind and leave with a plan of action!

Step One: Brainstorm Your Book Idea

I like to start each project with a brainstorming session, but first, I take some time to meditate, light a candle and set an intention to gain clarity around my book idea. If this is not in alignment for you, at least take some time to quiet the mind and go within. Perhaps take a walk in nature or do something that evokes inspiration.

Next, it's time to begin. Grab a sheet of paper and start by writing down your main idea or premise. Record any words or phrases that come to mind, and include everything that surfaces without stopping to re-think your ideas. Either make a list of your thoughts running down the page or start with your main concept in the center of the page in a bubble. As each new thought strikes, create another line or add each additional idea in a new bubble. Each branch that shoots off from your main idea may become a section or chapter in your book, but don't worry about structure just yet. At this point, you want to write freely whatever words or phrases enter your mind. Don't stop to second-guess yourself, just jot it all down. It may not make much sense at the time but through word association, it may spark another idea, so it's important to write freely without interrupting the creative flow.

Step Two: Compile a Loose Outline to Organize Your Thoughts

Now that you've taken some time to get clear on what you want to write about, and you've brainstormed your topic to further develop your ideas, it's time to craft those ideas into a book. The best way to flesh out your ideas and create a roadmap for your writing journey is to create a loose outline. In my experience, the thought of creating an outline is often what stops aspiring authors in their tracks. Do not let the thought of creating an outline kill the forward-moving progress you just worked to create in the previous exercises. We create an outline not to enforce structure and discipline, but as a way to help you organize your thoughts, and build a template for your book. As you're writing, there will be times when your book will likely take on a life of its own, and you may veer off track from your initial plan. Resist the urge to stop the flow of creativity just because it isn't what you initially set out to create. When the book begins to develop, see where it takes you. If you lose your way or get stuck, that's when you'll want to reference the outline to help you regroup, collect your thoughts, and get back on track.

Take your insights from your brainstorming session and start to put your chapter ideas in a logical order, either on paper or by using note cards. Again, don't get too hung up on structure because you can always move sections and chapters later during the revision process. For now, we just want to create a roadmap for the journey ahead.

For each chapter, list the title and then add three to five bullet points for each. You might also decide to repeat step one and conduct a brainstorming session for each chapter individually to further develop your thoughts.

Once you have as many chapters as you can think of, add a few bullets for your Introduction, which should tell who you are and how this book came to be. In your Conclusion, summarize your message for the book and leave your reader inspired to take action. That's a good start for now; later you can add the Dedication, Acknowledgments, Endorsements, Appendixes, About the Author section and a strong Call-to-Action page.

Step Three: Create a Plan of Action

If you know the type of book you want to write, and you know the average word count of that style of book, the next step is to decide on a date when you would like to have your first draft finished so that you can estimate your target daily word count (T.D.W.C.).

The first step in finding your target daily word count is setting a goal for the final word count of your manuscript. To help you with this, I've added a table of average word counts for various types of books.

WORD COUNTS FOR VARIOUS TYPES OF BOOKS:

Short Stories: 7,500 words or less

Novelette: 7,500—17,500 words

Novella: 17,500—40,000 words

Novel: 40,000—90,000 words

(between 50,000—70,000 is average)

How-to eBook: 25,000—40,000 words

Non-fiction/Business: 40,000—70,000 words

For example, let's say you plan to write a non-fiction book of 40,000 words, and you would like to complete the first draft within 90 days. You'd simply divide 40,000 words by 90 days, and now you know your target daily word count is 444 words. This means if you stick to your commitment of writing 444 words per day, then you can have your first draft completed in just 90 days. Even though I feel confident you could accomplish this goal by simply setting aside one hour of writing per day, you may feel that you need more time. No problem! You can use this formula to find your target daily word count based on a timeline that works best for you:

__ (Goal Word Count) divided by __ (# of writing days) = __(T.D.W.C.)

Finally, I like to keep a spreadsheet on my desk and keep track of my word count each day. This way, if I miss a day or fall behind, I know exactly how many words I need to make up when I have more time. By sticking to this plan, you will stay on track to reach your book-writing goal by your projected completion date.

Are you ready to tell your story? Give these tips a try. Find a quiet space; somewhere free of distractions. Place your hand on your heart, close your eyes and set an intention for your writing session. Finally, take a deep breath and allow the heart to lead the way. You may be pleasantly surprised by what you create!

CHAPTER

Twenty-One

Recovering The Grieving Heart
By Talia Renzo

TALIA RENZO

At a young age, Talia was bullied tremendously in school. Her dad passed away unexpectedly. As she experienced great loss, it brought her to a higher appreciation for wisdom. Talia decided not to fall the same way as everyone else did through life's greatest trials. Instead, she took all her pain and channeled it into passionate writing and pearls of wisdom. She wrote her first book at sixteen years old and has taken to writing for her healing and shares inspiration for others in need of love, healing, and wisdom. Visit her Facebook page for promotions and release dates: www.facebook.com/taliarenzo

Acknowledgments

For my beautiful past, present, and future readers all around the globe. Thank you for reading alongside my journey, as I will always continue to support you in yours. Thank you to my dad. I feel him and his love with me each day. Thank you for always watching over me and blessing me with such a beautiful inspiration of poetry. Thank you to all my friends and family. I am grateful for you every day. Thank you all from the bottom of my heart for the words of encouragement, laughter, motivation, and love. A big special thank you to Ann Albers, Sunny Dawn Johnston, Kim Richardson, and Kyra Schaefer for giving me wings to fly in my life. For my love, Garrett; I thank God for you every day. Thank you for loving my heart, and bringing me joy, and laughter every day.

Recovering The Grieving Heart
By Talia Renzo

T his book is about beautiful authors sharing their wisdom and expertise in walking the most difficult yet rewarding journey called life. Full disclosure: this chapter must be read with vulnerability. If you or somebody you know has experienced loss and is dealing with or has dealt with grief, you, my friend, are in the right place at the right time.

I have a theory that grief is more than the loss of a loved one. Its set of emotions can be experienced through bullying, sexual assault, the end of a valued relationship, and other traumatic events or variables of loss that induce different physical and emotional reactions. This natural response varies per individual. There is no wrong or right way to grieve. The pain will lessen with time. However, to fully grieve, you must do the footwork and experience what demands to be experienced to move forward, and live life after death.

Whatever grief you have today, will have a promise of a better tomorrow. As often as grief leads to depression, anxiety, abandonment, and trust issues, its power over you is not nearly as strong as your perseverance and determination to overcome its level of difficulty. No matter how timeless and impossible it may seem, you ultimately have the power to heal the wounds that were left open. I know all too well about grief, and it's known and even unknown powers.

When I was fifteen years old, my dad passed away unexpectedly in his sleep. At that moment, I began to live out my worst nightmare of hell, also known as grief. During the time of my father's transition, I was bullied physically and emotionally into silence in high school. After my dad died, the bullying persisted. My self-esteem was too far gone along with my identity. I eventually carried out my studies at home and found myself alone with my grief. I had no friends, no father, and I was shaken to the core by the amount of trauma that required attention. I analyzed and reviewed my options of what direction my life would go. I saw the coping mechanisms that were at arm's reach. I saw all the voids that could have been filled artificially, such as drugs and alcohol. I recognized the temptations of toxicity. I could have chosen toxic people, toxic relationships, and toxic decisions. At such a young age, I made the decision not to be the victim anymore. I no longer wanted to be in toxicity's company. I declared this decision organically, without any influences. I was no longer going to be the victim of bullying, the girl who lost her dad, and the girl with a million insecurities. I was going to construct a person behind my name.

I looked grief in the eye and saw fear looking back at me. Rather than being afraid, I took a deep breath and accepted the challenge of becoming fearless. I was committed to my battles. Little did I know that many of those battles would be me against myself. I fought depression, anxiety, and increments of fear. I traveled through various stages of grief. Each day, each hour was a toss-up between different emotions. I didn't know what I was going to get out of every day. I had no idea how many times a day I would cry, or if I would even laugh. I felt like I was reliving the same day every day, seven days a week. It came to a point where I finally looked around and made the change that was needed for me to start living my life, as my dad would have wanted me to. I made this decision mostly in his honor and eventually realized that I needed to do this for myself too because I deserve to live to the fullest, as he did. I needed to clear anything that was feeding a negative lifestyle. I focused on my wants, my needs, and learned to enjoy my company. Slowly but surely, I saw rapid improvement in my healing progress.

I wanted to heal badly, and I was determined to do so. I knew that the traumatic events that happened to me were not going to impact the way I was going to live out the rest of my life. So, what did I do? I took my power back. I took back the power of the piece of me that died with my dad. I took back the power that the bullies once took away from me. I took back my identity. I learned something that you can always carry with you. When you find yourself in need of taking your power back from someone or something that took it away from you, know that there is a fine difference between taking your power back versus making sure your power is never taken away from you again. This difference can go unseen.

When you take your power back, you can either leave it unclaimed or reclaim it as yours once again. The difference is that you can say, "I do not want to get hurt again," which doesn't sound reassuring. Or you can say, "I refuse to get taken advantage of in that way, by that person, by that event. I refuse for it ever to happen again because who I am does not deserve that. The person that I am deserves love," which is not only reassuring, but an affirmation for healing on its own. The decision is ultimately yours. Like with anything in life, your approach and your attitude will always reflect the outcome.

Grief sounds intimidating. It looks intriguing to avoid in its entirety. Grief is like having the flu. From a distance, it looks horrible and contagious. You would do anything you can to avoid it. Once you become grief's victim, some will offer their love and support for your healing, but others will avoid your contagion entirely. As heartbreaking as this experience can be, what I've learned is that everybody will experience a significant loss in their lives. We can't expect others to understand what we are going through. If they were sick, they would not expect us to understand the symptoms of their illness. It can be seen through a different focus, but everybody reacts differently on this journey. You must release all expectations of others and focus on the love that you already have. Most importantly, focus on the love that you have confided in yourself.

What many people don't know is that many rewards come with grief. When you experience any kind of loss, what is the most common question that we ask ourselves after we have had time to reflect on our loss? "Why did this happen to me?" There is an answer to that question. You're not going to like it, but the truth is not necessarily meant to be liked. The truth is, things happen to us to serve our highest good. The highest good is even being served to the ones that have passed on. From what I have gathered in life, everything always happens for a reason.

When our loved ones pass on, they never "die" because their spirit will live on forever in the same place their spirit was born, on this Earth. As difficult as this is to comprehend, their highest good is being served at this moment just as ours is being served right now. For those of you who don't know what your "highest good" is, our highest good is the best unknown outcome for our lives. We must trust the possibility and the philosophy that amazing things will happen. We must align ourselves with the best selves that we can be. Surely and steadily, we will reach our highest good on our path of life, and all hard work will be paid off.

Time lives on forever. It is not seen, but experienced. Our loved ones are infinitely experienced even when we cannot always see them. Time and grief are magnetic to each other's existence. To survive grief, you must embrace time and the premise of grief and its timeline.

What happens to us when our loved ones move on? We must move on also. It sounds impossible and almost unlikely, but I promise you, we have the power to move on. The first step to moving forward is accepting time. When you give yourself time to evaluate the past, the present, and the future, you immediately have the upper hand. Take time to feel the emotions of what happened. Sit with the experience and feel the emotions that demand to be felt. Let the flow naturally occur without force. Laugh when needed, cry until you cannot cry anymore, and most importantly, be present with the past. This may be the one time you're ever going to grant permission to look back on your past. No matter what you do, do not get confused, and let your past become part of your present. Leave your past in the past and move onto what you need in the present moment.

Where are you in the present moment? Notice your breathing, recognize your surroundings, count your blessings. Focus on right now. Where are you as you hold this book? How are you feeling? Take a deep breath and give yourself whatever it is that you need right now, whether that is a glass of water, another deep breath, or even a hug. Feel the power of this moment. Utilize this frame of time as a sacred and safe space. You are okay. You are breathing. You are well. Most importantly, you are healing. You are on the right track to a healed, positive, and happier self.

Once you feel like you have given yourself what you need in this present moment, let's move into the future. Sit with the idea of what your future will be like amidst this traumatic occurrence. As difficult as it is, try to see past this tragedy. See past the pain, the fear, the anger, and the grief. See the potential that lies ahead. Once you begin to envision a space for healing, make room in your heart for the endless possibilities for the life ahead of you. Reach into the deepest and darkest part of your heart and invite the warmth of healing. As exhausting and draining as these exercises can be, it's more exhausting not to practice them and be stuck in the tornado of grief. As impossible as it seems at this moment, make room in your heart for healing. I promise you, it can be done.

Grief is universal. It's one of the few types of emotions that can alter your brain chemistry. It demands to be felt and experienced in its entirety. As this may confuse those around us, appreciate them and what they can understand about it. Appreciate their love, embrace their presence, and spread kindness. Make sure to be kind to yourself, as you deserve it too. Whatever loss you experience in life, make sure you collect and count your blessings, moments of gratitude, and random acts of kindness. Carry these curations with you, as they will eventually become tools for you on your path through the pain.

Be kind to yourself. Your experiences do not define you, rather they are part of your journey and your story.

CHAPTER

Twenty-Two

Architect Your Life With
Empowered Dreams
By Dr. Vicki L. High

DR. VICKI L. HIGH

Dr. Vicki L. High is a best-selling author, founder of Heart 2 Heart Healing, life coach, counselor, speaker, and former mayor. Dr. High, a pioneer in spiritual healing, boldly journeys into new frontiers of healing, love, empowerment and spiritual insights. She shares wisdom through direct experience in healing, intuition, and spiritual realms. Her gifts empower her to connect ideas and concepts and create patterns for life and healing. She lives through her heart, honoring each person as an aspect of God–Source.

Vhigh4444@aol.com www.heart2heartconnections.us
www.empowereddreams.com @heart2heartprograms
@stoptraumadrama, @kalmingkids, @empowereddreams

Acknowledgments

I want to acknowledge the power of *unconditional love* as a catalyst for change in my life. I also want to thank Mom for being a great teacher and student. I love how people have touched my life in extraordinary ways. Thank you to Diane Sellers, Tina and Lon Morgan, Darlene Owen, Jamie Norman, Janene Cates Putnam, Mayza Clark, Stacey McGown, and my family in addition to a host of wonderful other amazing beings who fill my life with joy and love.

Architect Your Life With Empowered Dreams
By Dr. Vicki L. High

"What do I want to be when I grow up?"

As a healer and counselor, people continually ask me this question, searching for fulfillment. The trouble is, they are often in their forties, fifties, and even sixties, still craving that dream. One thing is certain: if they don't act, their dreams will remain unfulfilled. As the founder of Heart 2 Heart Healing, I know I can help people architect the lives they dream. People are not living passion-filled lives. Perhaps they are living someone else's dream. They may be listening to voices inside that tell them they will never be successful. They may fear being able to support themselves if they feed their entrepreneurial spirit. Perhaps they feel frozen around their hearts due to childhood trauma. The fear of failure is squawking louder than the small, still voice within their hearts. Is this true for you?

After pondering people's comments and listening to my heart, Empowered Dreams was created to address 13 areas of our lives. These aspects are vital to our emotional, physical, mental and spiritual health. What would happen if we used these 13 areas to plan the life you want to live? I call them the 13 Points of Light and Life.

1st Point: Love Your Whole Self; Love Yourself Whole

You must love yourself. Imagine that your love for yourself is the trunk of your tree of life. How supported are you? When you love yourself, you teach people how to treat you and build a strong foundation for all the other areas of your life. We struggle with the "junk in our trunk," so I was inspired to create Mini-Me Exercises to heal low self-esteem. These exercises are free, but powerful, and I offer them to help people heal emotional injuries. Emotion, our primary language, is what we need to heal. The exercises are available to help you dump your junk when you are ready. It's not easy, but it does heal those wounded places within your heart. When you complete the process, you are in a completely different space. Your life changes. Your healing begins and evolves with each completed Mini-Me. If you struggle with hearing these parts of you—relax. These are the voices that speak to you in your head.

2nd Point: Nature, Plants, Animals and the Environment

This area of your life helps you determine if your dream home is at the beach, the mountains, city life or a house in the country. Do you have a yearning to make a difference in animal rescue projects or global warming? What pets comfort and open your heart? If you have an affinity for rocks and crystals, is your dream home within access of a crystal mine or rock quarry to feed your passion? It's important to ask these questions so you know how you respond. These questions cannot be answered by anyone but you.

3rd Point: Health, Healing, and Movement

This introduces the practices and allows you to determine the choices you make to keep your physical body healthy and whole. It encourages you to make active, conscious decisions for traditional, allopathic medicine as well as healing modalities deemed alternative and complementary. Movement refers to the type of activity that keeps your body in shape. It can be a daily exercise regime at the local gym, kickboxing, swimming, yoga or dancing. You make active choices for nutrition and supplements—everything you need for a healthier life. These choices nourish not only your body, but also your mind and soul.

4th Point: Relationships

Relationships bring intimacy into our lives. It isn't just the spousal or significant other relationship, however. Connections to others are vital for our well-being. Relationships dance around the physical, mental, emotional and spiritual areas of our lives. In romantic relationships, we may decide to become physically intimate, but not share our thoughts, emotions or spirituality. This results in only a 25% intimacy level because it is limited to the physical relationship. We may begin to share thoughts about where the relationship is headed, but we keep our emotions sealed, perhaps because of past trauma and a need to protect our hearts from pain. This moves us forward to around a 50% intimacy level. Our spirituality and emotions are still uninvolved. Our intimacy levels are impacted by barriers we place to keep us "safe." As we grow to trust a partner, we decide to deepen the relationship and share emotions, allowing a move toward an intimacy level of 75%. As we share the soul and spirituality, we begin the quest for 100% intimacy. These are only examples, but that is the idea.

In a non-romantic relationship, the physical intimacy becomes less important, but the mental, emotional and spiritual issues become greater factors in how much of ourselves we are willing to share. How vulnerable and trusting can we allow ourselves to be?

If someone we trust violates a friendship, marriage, or family relationship, we erect barriers, distance ourselves, and even shut down communication to avoid addressing the hurt and disappointment. We often hide behind a mask of anger, shielding us from feeling fear, disappointment, frustration and hurt. If we communicate while wearing that mask, we are neither empowered nor speaking our truth.

One of the most important revelations in relationships is the flavoring that carries from old relationships to new relationships because of our history and energetic cords. Draining Relationship exercises (which are also free) on my website encourage you to explore and cut the cords that tie you and your new relationship to old issues. Have you ever realized a pattern in the partners and friends in your circle? It may be that the old energy patterns need to be swept clean to provide a new start for you! Become empowered, so that you can accept the quality relationships that honor and reflect the trust, love, and honesty you desire and deserve.

5th Point: Parenting/Mentoring

Parenting and mentoring provide awareness to the children who are being born and the younger generations who come with big purposes. They have been referred to as "Crystal Children" and "Indigos." There are other classifications, but this insight gives a parent the opportunity to learn more about these gifted children, the challenges parents face and the privilege of parenting them. These amazing beings are usually more aware of their gifts and will teach us, if we let them. These principles can also be applied in mentoring programs as we learn more about and listen to the voices that speak the truth.

6th Point: Spiritual Paths

Spiritual paths offer us the freedom to explore other religions. We may hear voices from our past that incite fear and stifle our freedom to explore and learn. When I found the courage to explore, I realized the more I learned about other faiths, the stronger I was in my own faith. I grew to appreciate unconditional love in all its forms: the wisdom of good works, the unification of a purpose, the quieted mind, the love of our beautiful planet and galactic citizenship. I learned that my relationship with God was my own, and I wouldn't trade my experiences. In accepting others and their spiritual paths, I lived the freedom of religion. It was no longer just a statement; I lived my inalienable right.

7th Point: Passion-filled Careers

Passion-filled careers are the jobs we would perform even if we were independently wealthy. When we think of what brings us passion, peace, and joy (along with challenge and success), we find it is doing what we love and sharing what we know. What lights the fuse within you to become a fireworks explosion radiating your light into the world? Whatever it is—do it! The world is waiting for you to empower your unique gifts, working smarter, not harder. It is time to shine!

8th Point: The Art of Creation

The art of creation acknowledges that inspired actions come straight from the sacred heart of God. It could be a book, movie, song or artwork. Whatever the creation, it is from a place of infinity. Write that novel or self-help book. Someone is waiting to hear your story! Create that sacred space in your home and realize your gift for interior design is an expression of your holiest work.

9th Point: The Energy of Money

The energy of money presents your relationship with money and how you interact with it. If you danced with money, would it be a waltz or tango? People have had varying results with the Universal Law of Rhythm (also known as Law of Attraction). What if the energy of money, particularly your dance with money, could be healed and redesigned to free up access to all the money you could ever want? If energy is unlimited, and everything is energy, why wouldn't unlimited funds be available? How will your relationship with money transform your life?

10th Point: Communication

Communication produces elements of how you share your message via websites, social media, television, books, movies and more. As you plan how your dreams will be realized, how will that be communicated to friends, family, clients, sponsors and more? Who will help you get the word out? Who will help you create new paradigms of communication? Imagine the impossible and your intention will make it happen before your eyes.

11th Point: Knowledge, Education & Spiritual Gifts

These help identify, design and implement new approaches to changing education in our country and the world. Learning continues to evolve in schools, businesses, and everyday life. It's time to invest in new learning models and begin to value contributions and spiritual gifts of every single student and employee. When we remove the stigma of "gifted people," everyone will be free to claim their unique collection of spiritual gifts. Everyone has them. You can freely be all you are, and that includes your special attributes. Only you can claim the gifts with your name on them!

12th Point: Communities and Service to the World

These define the connections you want to make, the communities where you share common interests, and how you share your wealth with the world. As you give back, what causes resonate within you? Which projects make your heart sing?

13th Point: New Discoveries, New Frontiers, New Paradigms with Legislative Impact

This is one of my favorites. When we escape the tyranny of other people's rules, we are free to explore new paradigms, new discoveries, and new frontiers. Heart 2 Heart Healing played a major role in my dreams. Legislators must recognize the power of medical miracles that heal without invasive solutions and are outside standard boxes. These new paradigms are life-changing. We deserve the freedom to explore new frontiers and the security of laws to support it rather than prevent it due to fear, misunderstandings and outdated ideology.

When you work this life plan, you skillfully architect your life, not anyone else's life—your life. Build the blueprint by listening to the still, small voice within, and your mind will blissfully help you form the structure and the pathways to living your best life ever. It will be your single greatest investment in discovering your purpose in the world.

Several years ago, the Empowered Dreams 13 Points of Light and Life was piloted at the invitation of a dear friend. She was an earth angel living in a rural town, ravaged by poverty, drugs, unemployment and small-town politics. She provided new beginnings to those recovering from drug addiction or recent incarcerations. When she asked me for more information about the program, and I explained the 13 points, she immediately said, "You have to do this program for my employees."

When I arrived for the event, I realized she had required her employees to attend. I met resistance. For this to succeed, I would have to connect and build trust with each employee. I used my counseling skills, Mini-Me Exercises, and Heart 2 Heart Healing. She granted me the freedom to schedule individual sessions before we tackled the program. I was humbled as these beautiful souls experienced breakthroughs, sharing the pain of childhood traumas that led them to drugs, crime, and feelings of worthlessness. One woman was taken to the orphanage as a child and was never taught to read. Another was the victim of rape and incest, keeping her secret until she opened her heart to me. One lost a spouse to cancer and chose to care for the stepchild who had no one else. These are my heroes. They didn't trust me to help them at first, but they rose above their fears and steadily they planned for new tomorrows. One student shared that her life had changed dramatically since the workshop. She was no longer a prisoner in her home and was living her dreams. Through empowerment, I've repeatedly seen victimhood cease playing a role in people's lives. My heart and life were changed by these experiences, for if these beautiful souls can empower their dreams, anyone can!

Be prepared for challenges from your friends, your family, your coworkers, and even the universe. Through this grand adventure, you and you alone determine your destiny. Once you decide to move forward, there is nothing that can stop your Empowered Dream!

Are you ready? Let's get started. Keep a journal and watch the changes coming your way!

1a. What do you do to love your whole self?

1b. Will you commit to dumping the junk in your trunk? If so, when? Name the date.

2. What calls to you in the environment—your happy place?

3. How will you nourish your physical body?

4. What relationships need attention in your life? What relationships feed your soul?

5. What parenting skills do you need to help guide your children or your inner child?

6. What intrigues you about another spiritual path and how can you explore it?

7. Are you fully engaged in a passion-filled career?

8. What is your vision to create? How will you bring that vision to life?

9. What is your dance with money? How can you engage more lovingly with money and attract more of it into your life?

10. What communication skills do you wish to develop for letting your message change the world?

11. How will you awaken your spiritual gifts and explore beyond the limits imposed until now? How will you be a change-agent in the current educational structure?

12. What causes complete you? What communities share your compassion and visions for the future? How will you give back to the world, people and pets who have given so much to you?

13. How will you remain open to new paradigms, new frontiers and new discoveries with an open mind? Will you be a voice in the legislature or in your community to promote positive change in the world? How will you change the world?

In closing, I recently heard Jesus speak, "Where you walk, I walk. Who you love, I love." Then he made me laugh when he said, "You've got this. We've got this!" Architect your life! You've got this! We've got this!

Final Thoughts From The Publisher

It has been a true honor to work with the life coaches in this and all our other incredible books. If you would like to join us on your authorship journey we would love to have you

Visit us at

www.asyouwishpublishing.com

We are always looking for new and seasoned authors to be a part of our collaborative books.

If you would like to write your own book please reach out to Kyra Schaefer at kyra@asyouwishpublishing.

Recently Released
Happy Thoughts Playbook
When I Rise, I Thrive
Flame and Sparkles: The Magic Within by Isaac Bowers
Healer: 22 Expert Healers Share Their Wisdom To Help You Transform
Selling Emotionally Transformative Services by Todd Schaefer
Up Coming Projects
The Alternatives: 22 Expert Alternative Practitioners Help You Heal In New Ways
Inspirations: 100 Personal Uplifting Stories For Daily Happiness
The Nudge by Felicia Shaviri
When Angels Speak: Angel Communicators Share Their Wisdom

44259159R00149

Made in the USA
Middletown, DE
05 May 2019